The
Family Business
A NEW GENERATION OF BELIEVERS

PAM STEVENSON

outskirts
press

Outskirts Press, Inc.
http://www.outskirtspress.com

ISBN: 978-1-9772-2848-2

Outskirts Press and the "OP" logo are trademarks belonging to Outskirts Press, Inc.

PRINTED IN THE UNITED STATES OF AMERICA

ABOUT THE AUTHOR

Pam Stevenson knows what it's like to run a small family business with her husband. Mindful of the lifelong struggle for balance between family, work, church and community, she took a journey into God's word to find answers. What does God want us to prioritize while we live on earth? What does it look like to be in His family?

Her practical approach to Biblical literacy invites us all to feast on an extra helping of God's word, especially the most challenging. After all, being part of His family involves growth, discipline and responsibility.

Active church member, speaker, and Bible study facilitator, Pam's passion is teaching women's Bible studies. She volunteers in the state correctional Substance Abuse Felony Punishment facility in Burnet, Texas, and formed the non-profit, Joseph's Hammer, to build a worship center for women in prison to pursue a relationship with God.

Find more books by Pam Stevenson by visiting her website at
www.pamstevensonbooks.com.

Dedications

To Glenn, my eternal sweetheart and best friend: For understanding and supporting me without questioning the outcome. Thanks for loving me with forever love.

To Cathi, my sister and soul-mate: Your sweet spirit is a picture of God's gracious nature.

To Blake, Caryn, Lisa, Brent and Brandon –for making this life on earth a joyful journey. I love being a part of your life.

To Bettina, who loved people, stories and laughter, and gave me a passion to write.

To all who read, critiqued or prayed over the years- and believed He could use me.

To the ladies who passed through our Bible studies at the Ellen Halbert Unit, Burnet, TX, and allowed me to share a pivotal time in their lives when God changed everything.

TABLE OF CONTENTS

ACKNOWLEDGEMENTS

The stories and sayings of the wise men and women in my life are woven into the fabric of my consciousness and language. I humbly submit this book for God's purpose, giving Him all the credit for orchestrating my life, finding a way to use me, and giving me the occasion to write a few things down "while it is still Today".

INTRODUCTION

I remember the day everything changed for me. I fell off a small ledge, crushed my wrist and lost the use of my right hand for several months. That one physical incident triggered a spiritual momentum shift, moving me to discover the Word of God for myself. God used those humbling days of pain and soul searching to show me that HE intended to use my hands if I would follow His instructions. As He drew me close for fellowship, His Spirit slowly revealed errors I had accumulated, and taught me how to cast them out, one by one. I hope to share His great love with you by reflecting on some of His most difficult teachings.

When you open this book and flip through the pages, you'll notice numerous excerpts from the Old and New Testament. Seek God's kingdom with me to question, wonder and imagine as we grow in His knowledge. An intimate daily fellowship with God always stimulates personal growth and change. I hope you fall in love with your Creator and His Son, Jesus, more deeply with each chapter.

Looking back, I'm grateful for my shortcomings and troubles and praise God for each one of them. Through my mistakes, God reveals His forgiving nature to me. If He had not permitted me to fall, I might not have slowed down enough to hear His voice so clearly; I might not have taken the time to write what He gave me.

I see Him working in all our deficiencies, patiently, powerfully. When He calls you near to reveal His nature, His perfect plan for your life comes into focus. Jesus invites you to tag along with Him while He works, teaching you the family business.

If you are reading these pages, I've already been praying for you. I'm asking God to bring you into His household and show you what you need to know during this season of your life. I pray that He will stimulate your hunger and thirst for the truth of His Word, so that you'll wake up early each morning desiring more. I confidently expect His blessings to overtake you as you listen for His voice and follow Him into the kingdom of heaven.

RELATIONSHIP WITH GOD

We live in an era of unprecedented hope and despair. Families struggle with moral issues and earnest seekers lose hope because of the harsh realities of life. Vaguely aware of a need for change, this gnaw in our soul quickens us for spiritual growth and prepares us to take new steps of faith.

I think that most people expect a lullaby instead of adventure when it comes to a relationship with God. We've all behaved like babies for too long. We want someone to sing us to sleep again and tell us that they'll take care of everything for us. When we expect comfort from our religion, complacency often replaces the true reassurance that comes from our Creator. Take a fresh look into the timeless insight that the word of God reveals about our interaction with Him. See what He planned for our earthly relationships and search for the essence of God's character to uncover your own identity as His offspring. His word calls us to action and reveals His consuming desire for our loyalty.

Sometimes reading the Bible makes us uncomfortable. As a Christian writer, I make no apologies for the information I find there. I must warn the good citizens of this wonderful new age of ours: The bigger the problem, the more unworldly and unreasonable the Biblical truth to fix it. Mysterious and poetic, it personifies living wisdom, as it cuts right to the heart of any question with a precision blade that somehow changes us into better people.

People now substitute Bible study with self-seeking seminars, self-help advice, and follow-the-leader methods. The most basic Biblical principles cause us to squirm a little. C.S. Lewis wrote, "A 'liberal' Christianity which considers itself free to alter the Faith whenever Faith looks perplexing or repellent *must* be completely stagnant. Progress is made only into a *resisting* material." [1] He called these topics we hesitate to discuss "repellent doctrines." We advance spiritually or physically, only when we apply tension.

Think about an athlete. We identify with the familiar concept of "no pain, no gain" as it applies to physical training. In the same way that an athlete stretches the muscles to develop them, we face resistant materials in scripture to build our spiritual muscles. Jesus calls us to follow Him, knowing that God rewards us with divine endorphins when we endure the race.

As we study the Bible together, please indulge me to begin with the most obvious and misunderstood concepts. We must first ask the politically incorrect "repellent doctrine" question: **"Which god will I serve?"**

Throughout history people have worshiped the god(s) of their ancestors. In our shrinking world, however, diverse cultures put forward a sort of religious buffet, where seekers choose different facets of plausible belief-systems to suit them. Unless you're rooted firmly in Biblical faith, this humanistic view that pervades the collective consciousness obstructs your relationship with a very real Father God. The sole purpose of our faith should be to find a way past religion and into the kingdom where we meet with Love Himself. He is the promise we hope for. He is the great reward of faith.

We'd all prefer to believe in a blended religion, where a great life force allows all good people to reach their highest level of spiritual accomplishment. If you trust in such a generic being or energy-force, regardless of your achievement level on that path, you accept selected quotations from the Bible without really knowing what God's word says in context.

---

1   God in the Docks by C.S. Lewis, Christian Apologetics, page 91

Even if you believe in the God of the Bible wholeheartedly, you may not fully understand that other gods exist. He will not be confused or blended with other gods, and gives us a direct path to Him through His word. I ask you to do some critical thinking as we explore what He says.

You shall have no other gods before Me. You shall not make for yourself a carved image—any likeness *of anything* that *is* in heaven above, or that *is* in the earth beneath, or that *is* in the water under the earth; you shall not bow down to them nor serve them. For I, the LORD your God, *am* a jealous God, visiting the iniquity of the fathers upon the children to the third and fourth *generations* of those who hate Me, but showing mercy to thousands, to those who love Me and keep My commandments.

Exodus 20:3-6

If other gods really exist, then we need to identify them as a matter of obedience to this First Commandment. The Hebrew people of the Old Testament knew exactly what this meant, but in our time, the politically correct agenda clouds this basic message.

God includes people of every nation in His loving plan, but He absolutely requires that they reject all other gods after they turn to Him. You may say that leaves out millions of people in this world of cultural and religious diversity. However, as I search for the truth, God's word tells me that His love reaches out to all nations and transcends such debate.

Praise the LORD, all nations; laud Him, all peoples! For His loving kindness is great toward us, and the truth of the LORD is everlasting. Praise the LORD!

Psalm 117:1-3 (NASB)

For now, I want to assume that you believe in God, the Creator of heaven and earth and all that's within it. God declares that we, His people, receive blessings when we put aside other gods and follow His

3

commandments. In short, He loves us, and would appreciate recognition of His love.

> **You shall love the LORD your God with all your heart, with all your soul, and with all your strength.**
> **Deuteronomy 6:5**

Our unreserved and wholehearted response to God draws us into His multifaceted nature, but we gain the freedom of such unconditional love through His Son, Jesus Christ. Without His Spirit, we're easily distracted by numerous methods of serving Him and other gods at the same time, regardless of our sincerity. Our true purpose comes to light when we set our hearts on Jesus, who came to earth for a specific reason: to destroy the works of the devil.

> **Little children, let no one deceive you. He who practices righteousness is righteous, just as He is righteous. He who sins is of the devil, for the devil has sinned from the beginning. For this purpose the Son of God was manifested, that He might destroy the works of the devil.**
> **1 John 3:7-8**

The invitation to come into God's family extends to anyone who chooses to live according to His laws of love. We become joint-heirs through Jesus in the kingdom of heaven when we take part in destroying the works of the devil. His purpose becomes our purpose. Whether we acknowledge Him or not, the Bible also says that His life lights the way of all people.

> **In the beginning was the Word, and the Word was with God, and the Word was God. He was in the beginning with God. All things were made through Him, and without Him nothing was made that was made. In Him was life, and the life was the light of men.**
> **John 1:1-4**

If you search for meaning in this world, start with Jesus, the original source of light and spiritual power. It surprised me, a long-time Christian, when I considered how He must have loved this earthly sphere as it burst forth in the beginning. Picture His delight when the beauty of new life began to emerge. As the human family multiplied, surely He grieved to see people choose darkness and death over light and life. Imagine the angels looking on as Jesus volunteered to come to earth as flesh and blood to redeem His fallen loved ones. His willing sacrifice gave us the chance to choose life over condemnation.

He who believes in Him is not condemned; but he who does not believe is condemned already, because he has not believed in the name of the only begotten Son of God. And this is the condemnation, that the light has come into the world, and men loved darkness rather than light, because their deeds were evil. For everyone practicing evil hates the light and does not come to the light, lest his deeds should be exposed. But he who does the truth comes to the light, that his deeds may be clearly seen, that they have been done in God.

John 3:18-21

Eyewitnesses documented Jesus' miracles. When the temple leaders rejected Him and allowed him to be crucified, He ascended from the grave.[2] In that sacrifice, Jesus gave all people right of entry to the kingdom of heaven and His astounding love. He left behind the key to eternal life and proof that it's real. He sent us His Spirit as the Way to choose light over darkness. He teaches us reconciliation, bringing together people of all backgrounds and beliefs and continues to ask us to follow Him as peacemakers. But first we must die to our old self and set out on a new journey. Starting over, we're given a new identity as spirit beings, complete with promises beyond our understanding and the privilege to become children of God.

Jesus guarantees safe passage in the hidden heavenly realm. This is

---

2   John 20:19-20

where the real adventure begins. If you're not excited about your faith, get off the fence and come into the kingdom!

> **Therefore, from now on, we regard no one according to the flesh. Even though we have known Christ according to the flesh, yet now we know *Him thus* no longer. Therefore, if anyone *is* in Christ, *he is* a new creation; old things have passed away; behold, all things have become new. Now all things *are* of God, who has reconciled us to Himself through Jesus Christ, and has given us the ministry of reconciliation, that is, that God was in Christ reconciling the world to Himself, not imputing their trespasses to them, and has committed to us the word of reconciliation. Now then, we are ambassadors for Christ, as though God were pleading through us: we implore *you* on Christ's behalf, be reconciled to God.**
>
> **2 Corinthians 5:16-21**

Up to now, we've covered matters of the heart and mind. But when we choose to believe what God says, He expects us to make a move. Believers bear the distinct privilege of bringing people together with His message as we mature. God loves relationships and wants us to connect with each other and Him. He forgives our laziness and extends an invitation to join Him. Reach out in love and share this news: **"God was reconciling the world to Himself through Christ, not counting men's sins against them."** He did His part, and waits for us to do ours.

When we take this purpose seriously, we become children of God. Believing in Jesus, we take the first step and accept His love and mysterious grace. Our faithful words and actions merge into eternity and the Holy Spirit empowers us to deny old habits and grow exponentially.

Full reconciliation with God precedes the understanding we yearn for in our human relationships. As you listen for God's voice while going through a difficult time, don't think He's forgotten about you. We can easily identify with the story of the Israelites, trying to do what God instructed

6

them to do in the middle of a crisis.[3] They heard Him, yet wandered in the desert complaining about their circumstances instead of following His instructions. They failed to exercise their faith. Each time they came to Him for help, He responded with action.

He sent His word and healed them, and delivered *them* from their destructions.

Psalm 107:20

Hungry, thirsty and desperate for a change, they acted like rebellious fools. God satisfied their needs when they turned back to Him. He saved them from their distress after they prayed through their trouble. The good news of God's word gives us the strength to walk out of our spiritual desert and into the Promised Land as followers of the Way.

---

3   Psalm 107

PIERCE THE VEIL

If you trust, as I do, that our souls live on after we leave our earthly bodies, you contemplate the mysteries of an invisible world. Our destiny propels us into a hidden territory teeming with life. A thin veil now separates us from the warmth of our Creator and freedom as sons and daughters of God in the kingdom of heaven.

To learn of the significance of this veil, let's travel back in history to the days when Moses met with God on Mount Sinai. As the thousands of families waited at the base of the mountain, God revealed His requirements and commandments. These encounters with God caused Moses to literally glow! Imagine a shimmering light emerging from among the stony crags. The Israelites scattered when they saw that it was Moses, because they could not bear the brilliance of God's radiance reflecting from his face.

> **Now it was so, when Moses came down from Mount Sinai (and the two tablets of the Testimony _were_ in Moses' hand when he came down from the mountain), that Moses did not know that the skin of his face shone while he talked with Him. So when Aaron and all the children of Israel saw Moses, behold, the skin of his face shone, and they were afraid to come near him.**
> **Exodus 34:29-30**

First Moses called the leaders back to him, and then all the Israelites came near Him to hear the commands of the Lord.

And when Moses had finished speaking with them, he put a veil on his face. But whenever Moses went in before the LORD to speak with Him, he would take the veil off until he came out; and he would come out and speak to the children of Israel whatever he had been commanded. And whenever the children of Israel saw the face of Moses, that the skin of Moses' face shone, then Moses would put the veil on his face again, until he went in to speak with Him.

Exodus 34: 33-35

They understood that the glow reflected God's light, yet they seemed to need that shade-cloth over Moses' face after he spoke directly with God. It hurt their eyes to look at him. Years went by and many of the Israelites lost sight of God's very real presence among them because they could no longer see His reflection.

Clothing himself in flesh, Jesus, the Son of God, came to earth to reunite us with His Father. When He died on the cross, the priests reported that the heavy layered veil which separated the holy room where they kept the stone tablets ripped in half.[4] By His sacrifice He permanently removed our need for the veil.

For if what is passing away _was_ glorious, what remains _is_ much more glorious. Therefore, since we have such hope, we use great boldness of speech— unlike Moses, _who_ put a veil over his face so that the children of Israel could not look steadily at the end of what was passing away. But their minds were blinded. For until this day the same veil remains unlifted in the reading of the Old Testament, because the _veil_ is taken away in Christ. But even to this day, when Moses is read, a veil lies on their heart. Nevertheless when one turns to the

---

4   Mark 15:37-38

Lord, the veil is taken away. Now the Lord is the Spirit; and where the Spirit of the Lord *is,* there *is* liberty. But we all, with unveiled face, beholding as in a mirror the glory of the Lord, are being transformed into the same image from glory to glory, just as by the Spirit of the Lord.

2 Corinthians 3:11-18

While He walked the earth as a man, Jesus warned that the temporary physical world must not consume us. He confronted evil boldly, casting out demons from the sick and troubled people who reached out to Him. And by word and example, He taught us that our bodies should function as living temples of the kingdom of heaven while we're here.

Now when He was asked by the Pharisees when the kingdom of God would come, He answered them and said, "The kingdom of God does not come with observation; nor will they say, 'See here!' or 'See there!' For indeed, the kingdom of God is within you."

Luke 17:20-21

Further, He insisted that it takes a small amount of faith to begin growing and participating in this spiritual domain.

Another parable He put forth to them, saying: "The kingdom of heaven is like a mustard seed, which a man took and sowed in his field, which indeed is the least of all the seeds; but when it is grown it is greater than the herbs and becomes a tree, so that the birds of the air come and nest in its branches."

Matthew 13:31-32

We look at our circumstances, wondering how this could make any difference in our lives. We pray and get mixed results, just as the disciples when they found themselves unable to heal a boy. They asked Jesus why they failed.

So Jesus said to them, "Because of your unbelief; for assuredly, I say to you, if you have faith as a mustard seed, you will say to this mountain, 'Move from here to there,' and it will move; and nothing will be impossible for you. However, this kind does not go out except by prayer and fasting."

Matthew 17:20-21

Jesus fasted and prayed forty days. That's all we're told about the beginning of His ministry. I often wonder what He endured when He walked into the desert to conquer His flesh, ignoring the pangs of hunger and cold dark nights. He faced the devil, defeated the adversary when tempted, and put His body under the command of the Holy Spirit. He prayed and practiced.

When He said to move mountains with faith as small as a mustard seed, the obvious contradiction to logic may cause us to disregard the statement. Notice the ease with which He tells us "nothing will be impossible" for us. When we combine our spoken words with uncompromised faith, we hold the power to defy the world's perception of physics in a wink. Our Father prepares us for results through prayer and obedience. When we forget about ourselves, fasting from our pleasures and worries, becoming the container where God plants the mustard seed of faith, we eventually bear fruit. Our roots of conviction push through crevices of adversity to split the mountain of doubt wide open!

Relinquish your notion of being superhuman, super Christian, super Mom, or super whatever, and realize that He created us with tiny invisible particles by design. Your faith to believe, *really believe*, will not be disappointed if you move from the natural world to the spiritual kingdom of God to see how He operates.

We live in freedom when we cooperate with Him, yet that requires humility. Otherwise, we'd try to earn or force our way into His kingdom with our own man-made methods. To get beyond our doubts, we need the wisdom to seek only the truth, for upon close examination, we may find that our preconceived ideas about living in God's family may contain errors.

Nothing can prepare us properly for a spiritual journey. You may think that you don't have time to start today. Hesitation and fear lead to phantom excuses. You may worry that a spiritual journey requires vast religious knowledge and is a fundamentally complicated and mysterious matter. If you think you must first create the perfect environment, a less stressful atmosphere, I urge you not to procrastinate. Forget about your past and focus on your desire to seek the truth in God's word.

When Jesus prepared His disciples for His physical departure, He described exactly how they could carry on the miraculous works without Him.

Do you not believe that I am in the Father, and the Father in Me? The words that I speak to you I do not speak on My own *authority;* **but the Father who dwells in Me does the works. Believe Me that I** *am* **in the Father and the Father in Me, or else believe Me for the sake of the works themselves.**

John 14:10-11

Revealing the tender mercy of such a simple plan, He simply followed God's instructions and expects us to follow the same model. He explained how His powerful Spirit could direct us in the same way if we choose to live in Him. Think about it and relax in your relationship with the Father. Our spirits live in flesh, blood, bone and tissue as conduits for God's power when energized and connected to Him. Somehow the seed of faith ignites a spark in the heart and mind of the believer, and God extends His power to the physical realm in us. *Listen and obey immediately.* It couldn't be simpler. God created us to do His work and relate to Him in ways we do not yet understand. His desire to carry on the family business through our faith enables our own vision of purpose.

A little while longer and the world will see Me no more, but you will see Me. Because I live, you will live also. At that day you will know that I *am* **in My Father, and you in Me, and I in you.**

John 14:19-20

Have you seen a ripple in a pond? You know without question that the unseen activity below the surface is real, even if you can't see what created the ripple. Suppose you were to concentrate for a long time, trying to see into the water. You might occasionally see a fish or turtle rise to the surface. If you really wanted to know what happens below the surface, you might go underwater and open your eyes. You could then make your own ripple. But your physical body will always limit your capacity to see in the murky water.

Similar to the ripple on the water, God's voice reverberates in our soul and we actually see the effects of it when we listen and follow His instructions. On the surface we see the physical world surrounding us. As children of God, however, we learn to distinguish and discern spiritual activity as new beings with a new nature. Jesus calls us immerse ourselves in the kingdom to develop our relationship with Him while we live on earth. We represent a unique class of beings in God's kingdom, with the chance to live and breathe in our flesh for a short time.

God enables us to use His words and the force behind them when Jesus' Spirit rests in us. As His sons and daughters, we must mature enough to take responsibility for the power we hold. Until then, God allows us, His believers, to practice our faith, not fully understanding the mystery behind the authority of the word.

But as many as received Him, to them He gave the right to become children of God, to those who believe in His name: who were born, not of blood, nor of the will of the flesh, nor of the will of man, but of God.

John 1:12-13

Look closely. Christ gives all believers *the right to become* children of God. Our belief in Him starts the renewal process that marks the beginning of our eternal life. That rebirth brings us into the spiritual world where we increase in wisdom as He reveals our character to us.

He waits until we choose to open our hearts and minds to all that this power implies. Then His love nourishes us and His Spirit teaches us while we play at our faith. Imagine, not just eternal life, but eternal growth and purpose in the kingdom of heaven as we mature into sons and daughters of God. The spiritual kingdom within us operates under a strict set of laws; the King holds absolute control and authority. His Son instructs us and gives us tools to practice and develop there as spiritual citizens. We can start living eternal life now, while we're on earth, when we obey Him.

> **And He said to them, "Go into all the world and preach the gospel to every creature. He who believes and is baptized will be saved; but he who does not believe will be condemned. And these signs will follow those who believe; In My name they will cast out demons..."**
>
> **Mark 16:15-17a**

According to Jesus, believers hold the potential to demolish spiritual strongholds and cast out demons in His name. That's the first sign of a follower. Yet many believers remain in bondage to the flesh, not having taken this seriously. Freedom gradually takes hold when we practice our faith, taking the focus off of our own plans and hearing God telling us that we need to clean up our own house thoroughly.

Many teachers say that these signs disappeared after the apostles died. I've listened to their theories and rejected them, although their arguments are heartfelt and rooted in love for our Lord as they defend the faith they've been given. Indeed, if few in the church believe that the signs will follow, then that explains why the word "demon" creates such a shudder among Christians. Surely Jesus continues to encourage His followers, **"...these signs will follow those who believe..."** and when we ask why we're oppressed, He replies, **"...because of your unbelief..."** I am a simple person. I believe the Bible and every word of God. If a sincere teacher tells me something that does not match up with scripture, then I'll want to hear out their reasoning and test it against other scriptures. If they honestly seek the truth, we will respectfully mature together as we try to understand God's words.

Learning to recognize demons in our own life and dealing with them one by one, we learn to master the other profound teachings by following

Jesus. There's nothing to prove, no reason to create a stir or bring attention to ourselves. These signs will follow us when we believe. He calls us to become emissaries, kings and priests in the heavenly realm, proclaiming the good news on earth. What, then, are we waiting for?

ENTER THE KINGDOM

Find a straight pin and observe the head. That's the actual size of a mustard seed. You have nothing more important to do but hold onto that much faith for a few more minutes. Once you get the hang of it, you'll wonder why you stayed at the separation veil for so long.

Remember, if doubt starts to creep in, or if you begin to think that that God is too busy for the small stuff, just look at the pin and remember what Jesus said about moving the mountain of doubt that looms in your mind. Hang onto His words as you formulate your own. Show up to walk and talk with Him. Just as a mustard seed grows into a large tree, we can experience in increasing measure the majesty and power of the kingdom of God.

Many believers simply stop at the veil of separation, not understanding Jesus' words about the little seed. Some think that they must achieve a large faith before they can experience God's victory. However, with only a small measure of faith, I know better. You cannot control faith, but you can practice it and use this most precious gift from God, the key to eternal life and peace during this lifetime on earth. (And you know that keys are small.)

When we clear out our big ideas about faith, we simply surrender to the power of the Holy Spirit. Don't let hesitation creep into your mind about your worthiness to be in God's presence. Don't worry about how to approach Him. He loves you and hopes you won't give into distractions that harden your heart and keep you from following His instructions.

Therefore, as the Holy Spirit says: "Today, if you will hear His voice, do not harden your hearts as in the rebellion, in the day of trial in the wilderness, where your fathers tested Me, tried Me, and saw my works forty years. Therefore I was

angry with that generation, and said, 'They always go astray in their heart, and they have not known My ways.' So I swore in My wrath 'They shall not enter My Rest.'"

Hebrews 3:7-11

Poised to follow Him, I hold my Bible and say a prayer. "I belong in there with you, God. I want to know your ways. Sometimes I feel like a foreigner in this body of mine, but I want to reflect your glory like Moses. Transform me into your likeness. I want to move some mountains! I believe that Jesus opened the Way for me to live in Your kingdom. He lives in my flesh and will teach me to live in your perfect love right now."

I hear Him say, "Come in, my child, and rest with me. Bring your friends. I have something to show you."

Eagerly I take a small step. Come with me and glimpse the Creator of Love. As we hold onto our tiny pins of faith and close our eyes, we imagine that we pierce the veil. Light bursts through the miniscule hole and we begin to see where He's taking us, far beyond our religion, into His kingdom. God knows what we need. Immediately, a sense of well-being surrounds and penetrates us. Awash in pure joy, flooded with a sense of certainty, our deepest longings find fulfillment in the presence of the Creator. He shaped us for timeless joy. Let's claim it! We begin to realize that our thoughts about God do not change Him. Our efforts to define Him or clarify Him pale in the reality of His all-encompassing love.

Before we broke through this illusion of separation, we mistakenly believed that God's expression of greatness in our own lives hinged on our own measure of conviction. We thought that somehow we participated in the creation of miracles with our own confidence in them. We thought that our spiritual success depended on how big we made our faith. That single lie keeps many seekers away from the peace they hope for.

Now, just beyond the veil, we simply rest with God. He tells us that we need do nothing but let go of our own plans and allow Him to extend His graces through us. In this environment, we have access to the Holy Spirit who teaches us all things. We recognize that until now we tried to extend His grace *for* Him by a manifestation of our *own* faith. Our doubts melt away and we surrender to His peaceful renewal process.

When we agreed to take this spiritual journey to understand Him better, we tiptoed past that veil with some great need in our heart. God permeates every cell to know the deep matters of our hearts. He knows our shortcomings, but He hears our cry. Strangely enough, we maintain an overwhelming certainty that He loves us anyway!

> Paul prayed: **...that the God of our Lord Jesus Christ, the Father of glory, may give to you the spirit of wisdom and revelation in the knowledge of Him, the eyes of your understanding being enlightened; that you may know what is the hope of His calling, what are the riches of the glory of His inheritance in the saints ...**
>
> **Ephesians 1:17-18**

In an effortless moment, we experience the most holy place, the **kingdom of God**, tucked neatly away in our seed of faith; larger than life, yet so small it cannot be seen by natural eyes. But the peace found there today is real. It represents a repellent doctrine to all learned men who lack vision and refuse to go there.

See within yourself a world of possibilities for your communication with God. Go to the temple and worship at the feet of your Creator. It stands within you as a protected plane of higher learning in the spiritual world. When Jesus talked to Nicodemus about the kind of wisdom we seek, He knew that we could not grasp it all at once. He knew we would need to sit daily at His feet in the temple of our heart, listening and learning.

> **If I have told you earthly things and you do not believe, how will you believe if I tell you heavenly things?**
>
> **John 3:12**

Our hearts begin to pump harder as our brain tries to log this information where we can find it again as we look up from our chair and see that the clock has moved. We savor the moment and then shift back to the physical demands of the day.

Saturated with grace, drenched with a peace that does not match our physical circumstances, we get up and move about with a confident smile. Although it requires minimal effort, our obedience to take that humble step toward Him causes us to glow with God's light. When we seek the kingdom, we see the difference in our own lives. Follow Him there as often as possible to worship and learn.

THE NARROW PATH TO PEACE

Some may ask, "How do you remain calm in the midst of these circumstances?"

Inevitably, we all encounter a person or situation that distracts, irritates, or completely knocks us flat. Learn to expect it because we live in a fallen world. I don't know why it surprises us, but we have a habit of being disappointed about the imperfection of this human cycle.

Often we focus on the situation as if we must do something. Our "fight or flight" mechanisms trigger a response as our bodies gear up to either run or defend ourselves. The problem compounds in our mind as we play out the scenarios, trying to determine the right course of action for a faithful person. Our muscles tense as the darkness of doubt gradually overshadows our peace.

This kind of anxiety accumulates as we find ourselves stuck in traffic, stuck in a job, stuck in an addiction, stuck in any situation. We can't fight or flee, so we think our whole body must sit there stewing in its own juices! We begin to search for ways to ease the pressure of this cycle. These remedies range from self improvement introspect to intellectual debate; from prescription drugs and alcohol to illegal drugs. We take wholesome things like exercise, sex, food, work or good deeds, and obsess about them until they turn into the devil's distraction. How often we just turn to our favorite television show to "relax." These diversions replace the distractions that triggered the response that caused us to lose our peace. But they bring only more distraction.

We want to hold onto that peace that fills us when we enter God's Rest. Until we choose to filter our own thoughts through God's law, we cannot find lasting peace. Allow Jesus to wash away those anxious patterns of thinking. He gave us His indwelling Spirit to break the cycle.

Or do you not know that your body is the temple of the Holy Spirit *who is* in you, whom you have from God, and you are not your own? For you were bought at a price; therefore glorify God in your body and in your spirit, which are God's.
1 Corinthians 6:19-20

Ask Jesus to tell you what you need to know. Go directly to the source of all that is good and right and let Him begin to transform you, even if it hurts. He simply must get to the truth of every matter to heal it.

Do not think that I came to bring peace on earth. I did not come to bring peace but a sword.
Matthew 10:34

Jesus knows we live in a worldly cycle of disappointment, but He calls us to carry His light into a dark spiritual world. It involves an inner work of the mind and heart instead of a change in circumstances. God often uses our predicaments to get our attention or give us a lesson. Suppose you carry around a deep hurt from the past, not realizing that it affects your behavior. Follow Christ into the kingdom and He'll lead you straight to it, helping you use the sword of His word against that spirit. His love compels us to root out the conflicts that keep us from loving fully.

Therefore submit to God. Resist the devil and he will flee from you.
James 4:7

The minute we get up and move around on the material plane, the desire to control our physical circumstances applies tension to our spiritual development. The repellent principle of **subordinating our plans to God's will** appears ridiculous to a faithless person. We constantly negotiate with God for the power over, at the very least, our own little corner of the world. We often refuse to retrain our minds to match up with the thought patterns of our Creator.

Look into your heart and root out the conflict between your will and God's. These are demons resisting . Purify your temple and throw those little devils out as you recognize their errors. You can and must make choices about your own spiritual well-being. Read God's word to know the difference.

But seek first the kingdom of God and His righteousness, and all these things shall be added to you.

Matthew 6:33

The wisdom of the world took me on a long, restless search for success, comfort and accomplishment. When I began to read the Bible again, it saved my life and turned me onto the path of complete peace. His word actually rebukes and corrects us in our own private meeting with our Father.

LORD, my heart is not haughty, nor my eyes lofty. Neither do I concern myself with great matters, nor with things too profound for me. Surely I have calmed and quieted my soul, like a weaned child with his mother; like a weaned child *is* my soul within me.

Psalm 131:1-2

God requires that we give Him complete dominion over our lives. He sustains us physically. Yet He wants us to develop spiritually as He nourishes our souls. We prefer to think that we have our own ideas and we fiercely defend them. But look around. You have accumulated ideas from your life experiences and from other people. Your biases and mental habits make up your personality.

Do you have a little voice that repeats the same negative ideas in your head when you encounter a problem? Allow Jesus to provide the peace that keeps them out permanently and aligns you with the wisdom of God for your circumstances. Do you follow a pattern of panic, disappointment or fear when something goes wrong? Allow God to reprogram you to respond with His insight and purpose instead of calling upon your old habits.

> **Therefore I say to you, do not worry about your life, what you will eat or what you will drink; nor about your body, what you will put on. Is not life more than food and the body more than clothing?**
>
> **Matthew 6:25**

The importance you place on your self and your surroundings greatly impacts your spiritual expansion. There's nothing wrong with having good things around you, but God expects you to search the spiritual realm and realize that He offers much more than meets the eye. Solomon, the richest and wisest man of history wrote,

> **So I became great and excelled more than all who were before me in Jerusalem. Also my wisdom remained with me. Whatever my eyes desired I did not keep from them. I did not withhold my heart from any pleasure, for my heart rejoiced in all my labor; and this was my reward from all my labor. Then I looked on all the works that my hands had done and on the labor in which I had toiled; and indeed all *was* vanity and grasping for the wind. *There was* no profit under the sun.**
>
> **Ecclesiastes 2:9-11**

Even in the best of times, the fruits of our labor reflect only a small part of our true identity as spiritual citizens. When economies and nations fail, the Bible tells us to remember that earthly treasures give us no security whatsoever.

Christians today flock into congregations where there's very little accountability, desiring to participate in the life of the church without a commitment to grow in maturity. We start out with the intent to follow God's direction, thinking we'll learn how to do it in church. But instead we settle for entertaining worship services, meetings and programs, an assortment of shortcuts to knowing God in a busy world. There, we make plans *about Him* and *His church* or we participate in traditions *about Him*. In contrast, when we seek the kingdom of God and His righteousness, He launches us on a far-reaching journey, where we follow closely on the heels of Christ, learning His ways intimately. Then when we come together with our brethren, our love unites us as we sharpen each other with truth.

To grasp the deeper meaning of God's plan in your life, first find your place in the kingdom. Remove the cobwebs from your temple within, go in and spend some of your valuable time there. Ask questions in prayer if you are not sure where to start. Listen and wait to hear God's voice if you sincerely want to know what He expects of you. Get rid of the old ways you accumulated and purify yourself as you learn. Repent as you recognize what you've been keeping in there. Throw out those disobedient spirits. After that, God will invite you to put the truth into action as part of His chosen family, the body of Christ. This ongoing activity marks the life of a follower of the Way. Don't drift along or set out on your own. Follow Jesus when He tells you:

These things I have spoken to you, that in Me you may have peace. In the world you will have tribulation; but be of good cheer. I have overcome the world.

John 16:32

Observe a conversation between Jesus and Peter to get a better idea of how He'll teach you there. When Jesus asked, "Who do you say that I am?" Peter answered,

You are the Christ, the Son of the living God.
Matthew 16:16

Most people thought Jesus was a powerful prophet, but Peter had spent enough time to know that He was the anointed One. Jesus commended him and blessed him because:

Flesh and blood has not revealed this to you, but My Father who is in heaven.
Matthew 16:17b

Jesus wants us to communicate directly with His Father, and He went to extreme measures to teach us how to do it. He told Peter that He would build His church on this kind of spiritual revelation, whereby all men who desired to communicate with the Father could actually hear Him. After all, if He could hear the Father, then we should be able to hear the Father too.

...and on this rock I will build my church, and the gates of Hades shall not prevail against it.
Matthew 16: 18b

He knew that His Spirit would protect this family of newborn believers and hold the church together as one body. His Father would reveal spiritual insight, instructing each person individually as they heard Him speak. He described a picture of God's vision for the members of the church as they obeyed the Father's voice:

And I will give you the keys of the kingdom of heaven, and whatever you bind on earth will be bound in heaven, and whatever you loose on earth will be loosed in heaven.
Matthew 16:19

When we talk about heaven, we try to separate it in our mind as the afterlife. Pause and consider Jesus' words to straighten out any erroneous ideas you have about that. God plans to reveal your part in the process of binding and loosing *on earth*! He invites you to participate in heaven here and now.

Jesus began to describe to the disciples His death and resurrection and Peter responded with grit and determination, holding onto his own idea of the Messiah's purpose. Because he had just received special knowledge from God about Christ, he felt it appropriate to take Jesus aside and say:

Far be it from You, Lord; this shall not happen to You!
Matthew 16:22b

Jesus immediately gave him an important key to the kingdom in His reply. He turned and said to Peter,

Get behind Me, Satan! You are an offense to Me, for you are not mindful of the things of God, but the things of men.
Matthew 16:23

Did you notice the fragile fleshy membrane that separates us from the mind of God? Put yourself in Peter's place to understand it. One minute you hear a word from God, and the next thing you know, Satan tries to put words in your mouth and brings you back into the flesh to make plans *for* God. Jesus' response shows us how to calmly stay on the path of peace. We too, shall command devils to go, and expect them to obey quickly.

A word of caution before you rush out and start rebuking demons in other people: Jesus responded audibly because He wanted to teach His disciples. Notice that He did not speak to Peter, but saw and spoke directly to the disobedient spirit. Jesus taught Peter that no matter how earnestly he followed in His footsteps, Satan would continue to test and tempt. Watch for that devil and tell him to get behind you! If someone asks you to pray for them, then use it as a chance to share God's love and teach them to recognize Satan's meddling spirit.

Identify the spiritual adversary when he interferes with the things of God, even if his words come out of the mouth of a believer, and especially if they come out of your own mouth. Watch for him. He's offensive to the children of God and we should learn to smell him coming. He's learned to blend into the world, but we must discern between good and evil if we are to hear God's voice.

Confront your own demons and keep your own spiritual house clean. Build a protective wall of righteousness in your kingdom, where you can safely rest and learn from Jesus. Overcome the enemy within you and love one another. Instead of pretending you're without sin, outsmart that devil that's been tricking you and crush it. In time, when you learn to overcome the spirits, you'll walk with inner peace. Your obedience to stay on the path, no matter how steep the climb, gives you authority on earth to turn large problems into trivial matters. It's the key to discernment.

Your church body represents God's family; diverse participants form a spirit of love and truth, each one a special tool for His purpose. God expects us to build disciples who know His word and practice discernment of the devil, spurring each other on to maturity in faith. We should recognize that gradually over the centuries, deceivers have infiltrated our churches, too. For every truth-filled teacher around you, you may find another who has watered down scripture to make their message more readily acceptable. Others hold fast to doctrines without a spirit of reconciliation and love. Many believers accept basic teachings passed down through the ages without listening to God. Therefore, we cannot always believe what another man tells us about God's will for our lives.

A good rule of thumb: love one another, despite your sins, with a willingness to repent when you discover your own error. Hopefully the others in your church body are learning to do the same thing. In this way, we clean our spiritual houses together and become a holy community, truly set apart. We want to be **mindful of the things of God**, knowing that Satan tells us to make plans based on **the things of men**. Let's renew our commitment to defend the faith and search His word to confirm the truth.

We need God's council, with Jesus as our mediator. Set up a meeting. Knock on the door. Tell Him what's on your mind. Listen when He speaks, and confirm it through the Holy Scripture. Just do it and you'll learn to recognize His voice. You may feel a little silly about having a meeting with someone invisible, until you come out feeling like you've experienced a healing in your soul.

Ask, and it will be given to you; seek, and you will find; knock, and it will be opened to you.

Matthew 7:7

Many believers miss out because they get stuck in the asking phase, without sound teachings that lead to maturity and peace in the kingdom. They want eternal life after they die, but cannot imagine spiritual power for Today. God calls us to take some time for seeking in His kingdom and knocking on closed doors of His mystery to learn from the Master.

Long after Jesus removed the need for the veil of separation, we continue to expect it in our religion. We want our faith to be measurable, to fall under the controlled environment required by human intelligence. Yet the Bible tells us that faith is hope for things unseen. We find it much more comfortable to discuss and analyze religion as a thing set apart from us, than to live with a raw powerful faith teeming inside of us all the time. We either don't trust ourselves with it or prefer not to take the responsibility. Or maybe we just don't know how to start. Human nature prefers to hold God at a safe distance and bring Him into our life on our own terms.

Somewhere in religious history the veils of separation were added back in the church. It was the only way to appeal to the masses who could not take the unworldly claims of Christ at face value. The priests and pastors intermingled traditions and faith. Over the ages, churches and institutions built up beautiful structures as well as humble meeting places, each one staking their claim at the curtain of separation. Religions and denominations continue to train godly men who set out to follow Christ and preach the good news, but the worries of this world weigh them down. Some try to manage the church like a business with ever increasing creativity to appeal to newcomers and address the needs of budding believers. Spiritually lukewarm people line up on Sunday mornings with their tin cups to receive their ration of faith for another week. I know because I sat there, too, watching, listening, smiling, hoping, praying.

I refuse to sit still and watch any longer. I procrastinated long enough.

I'm listening for God, feeling His love for the people of His church in every breath of His Spirit. I hear Him saying not to leave anyone out, to go out in the streets and show His goodness to our enemies without concern for our own safety. I hear Him urging us to rebuild our spiritual walls, for they are in ruins[5]. With a spiritual sword in one hand, and a trowel in the other, we find our destiny. Jesus urgently calls the hungry and thirsty seekers among us to come on into the kingdom. The kingdom of God represents His power and authority, not just an invisible locked door He opens at the hour of our death.

When we advance in the spirit, Satan tells us that we must attain perfection. The world suspects fanaticism. Almost everyone calls us back to the veil for our own safety. Meanwhile, Jesus waits as the quarrels break out among us. In our time, Jesus calls us, the unworthy, to get out of the crowd and follow the narrow path to His peace. Then, show others the Way to the door of the kingdom.

I am the door; if any one enters by me, He will be saved, and will go in and out and find pasture.

John 10:9

If we enter the spirit world by Jesus, He offers protection against any deceiving spirits who try to trick us or dilute our faith. He leads us deep into the kingdom to a lush green pasture, so that we hear His word in safety. We spend time with Him there, taking what we learn into the challenges that come up daily. The prophets of old shared their insight of the realm where spirits dwell. Jesus gave us specific instructions regarding our authority and role as sons of the kingdom. However, people feel like they must choose one over the other: Physical vs. Spiritual.

Surprisingly, some people still believe that their physical body and surroundings represent the only reality. Science tells us that all things and all beings are composed of infinitely small cellular structures. Infinitely, meaning that we don't possess the technology to get to the bottom of it yet, but have a tiny glimpse into the mystery. Our own vast universe stretches

---

5   Nehemiah 2:17

out into unseen. Our physical world undeniably links us to the truth that we are wonderfully made. I don't care if God seems invisible; I want to dwell with Him now. If Jesus wants us to exercise our faith in His kingdom, we simply cannot ignore Him any longer.

YOUR TRUE IDENTITY

Fear of the unknown sets the stage for our limited understanding of the spirit world and makes it a repellent topic for believers. Yet the spirit world, our eternal home, contains our true identity.

> **It is the Spirit who gives life; the flesh profits nothing. The words that I speak to you are spirit, and *they* are life.**
>
> **John 6:63**

If you want to revitalize your life, look in God's word for wisdom. You'll see His plan for you as a part of the bigger picture. The world creates a perverted slant on scripture, either diluting the truth or casting doubt. If you want to know how your Father works and thinks, just open the Bible and see for yourself. It reveals something new each time you approach God saying, "I need your word and ask that you write it on the tablet of my heart. Prepare me for my time on earth. I praise you for ....."

God loves you and wants to hear these things from you. He'll listen to you when you repent and humble yourself before Him. Our obedience to read His word triggers spiritual activity and you might know that it involves a piercing!

For the word of God *is* living and powerful, and sharper than any two-edged sword, piercing even to the division of soul and spirit, and of joints and marrow, and is a discerner of the thoughts and intents of the heart.

Hebrews 4:12

Invisible spiritual battles encompass our globe, whether we know it or not. As eternal creatures with temporal needs, people search for a happy balance, vaguely aware of the spiritual aspect of life. When we turn to the Bible for clues, the knowledge changes us forever. Get past the veil of separation often and begin to see this world in a new light. Stop right now. Be still and listen for His voice.

"Love Me first," He speaks softly.

Open the Bible out of obedience and prepare to be amazed as you find exactly what you need today. A chill runs up your spine as you realize that God, Himself, speaks to *you*. Your Creator wants a relationship with you. He does not desire a one-way communication where His love falls like snowflakes on a hardened, unknowing ground. No, His word nourishes and sustains life itself. When you take it in, you produce righteous fruit.

For as the rain comes down, and the snow from heaven, and do not return there, but water the earth, and make it bring forth and bud, that it may give seed to the sower and bread to the eater, so shall My word be that goes forth from My mouth; it shall not return to Me void, but it shall accomplish what I please, and it shall prosper *in the thing* for which I sent it.

Isaiah 55:10-11

Although you live in the physical realm, you sense there's something more. God calls you heavenward to His side for reassurance of His protection. If you find yourself stuck or frozen somewhere along your spiritual journey, come near to the warmth of Jesus' light as He covers you with love and thaws your hardened mind. He may focus His light with laser precision, cutting out the cruelty of your worst fears to heal your broken heart. He will meet you where you need Him.

Today God sends forth His word to accomplish His purpose in every detail of our lives. He rejoices when we cooperate with Him, regardless of our past mistakes. As He teaches us, we begin to completely fall in love with Him. Our souls take on the shape of His Spirit and we discover our forgiven self, a little at a time. He celebrates with the host of heaven as we turn our lives over to Him day by day, moment by moment, until at last there is no more need for measuring time at all! We live, eternal beings, the offspring of our Almighty Creator.

We start out with the knowledge that Jesus loves us enough to lay down His life for us. He asks that we lay down our own life and follow Him into the kingdom of God, an invisible place inside our seed of faith. If we have, at some point in our lives, misplaced our seed, He opens the storehouse of plenty and plants a new one in our heart.

As we grow into a more mature friendship with God, He showers us with gifts of encouragement. He fertilizes and waters our seed each time we open the Bible. Just as a flower naturally opens to the sun, we open our minds to God's word and learn what He wants from our relationship.

The entrance of Your words gives light; It gives understanding to the simple.

Psalm 119:130

If you don't think you can understand the words, simply open the book of Psalm and sing His praise, vent frustrations, or wonder about His wisdom. You learn in Proverbs that God has a sense of humor – and infinite patience- to desire a relationship with us.

If you have studied God's word all of your life, you continue to find new insight in the words. Although the full depth of mystery remains undiscovered, one gets the feeling that we'll experience new aspects of this wisdom throughout eternity. The ancient Hebrew sages believed that the written laws of scripture represent the outer layer, the "garments", of the word of God. They taught that material beings could not survive an encounter with the unshielded Torah, and that the original Hebrew language was the "Holy Tongue". The twenty two letters of the Hebrew alphabet, some thought, contained the building blocks of creation as God breathed the physical universes into existence by speaking them.

Whether we believe in such a mystical view of God's word makes no difference to Him. However, each time we open the sacred book we delight our Father because it supernaturally opens the channel of communication. He teaches us as much as we can bear. The words form our reality when we speak them with faith and take them as our own identity. Open your mind to God's laws. Follow the steps of Jesus in the book of Matthew and try to touch His robe. See the truth revealed in the miracles and parables. God's word made flesh, pure love visible in the form of a human man, Jesus shared stories of the mystery of the universe He created. He stooped to touch, heal, feed, and teach about sacrifice and mercy. He felt our pain and understood our fragile physical balance between suffering and happiness.

He still cares. He knows how completely jammed our signals can get down here in the world where Satan freely roams. He came to teach us how to overcome these demonic spirits. God pursues the untamed spirit, not to tame him, but because He created him in His own likeness.

As for me, I will see Your face in righteousness; I shall be satisfied when I awake in Your likeness.

Psalm 17:15

His own likeness.... No matter how broken we feel, our transformation comes with a guarantee of eternal life. But we have to choose and accept complete forgiveness; otherwise, we'll die without Him.

Christ says, *"You are mine and I will never leave you."* His love exemplifies what we want in an earthly relationship. We want to be desired. We want to be pursued. We want someone to cherish us. We want to rest without any self-consciousness. We want to be understood and comforted when our souls tire of this world. We want to receive all the benefits of God's compelling love. Imagine His patience as He allows us to come to Him at our own speed, finding our way to Him at last.

Toddlers in the Kingdom

It may seem to God that we play peek-a-boo behind our earthly facade. I can just imagine God and His heavenly host cheering for us as we toddle along, struggling to carry our seeds of conviction. He looks forward to our growth. I sometimes wonder if He finds us, as believers in our times, spiritually retarded when He planned for us to be gifted. Only a few of us mature to our full divine potential.

> **Beloved, now we are children of God; and it has not yet been revealed what we shall be, but we know that when He is revealed, we shall be like Him, for we shall see Him as He is.**
>
> **1 John 3:2**

In God's eyes, we live as His children on this earth. Our Father winces each time we fall, draws us to Him for comfort, and delights in each small accomplishment. He knows that our actions may bring another soul back to Him. He invites us to listen and learn, increasing in spiritual strength as we live here on earth. We need exercise and practice to overcome the fleshy distractions and find our place of service.

The heart, that spiritual muscle that beats the rhythm of our days, seeks a healing. Perhaps someday scientists and doctors will describe which neurons and transmitters in the brain connect to our sense of well-being in the heart. For now, and forever, we can look to our Creator with complete confidence in our spiritual health.

> **The Spirit of the Lord GOD *is* upon Me, because the LORD has anointed Me to preach good tidings to the poor; He has sent Me to heal the brokenhearted, to proclaim liberty to the captives, and the opening of the prison to *those who are* bound.**
>
> **Isaiah 61:1**

We receive something unique and amazing each time we turn to God for answers. He enjoys us when we finally realize that He speaks to us

ALL THE TIME. When we open our hearts to know God intimately, our hope comes alive.

Now faith is the substance of things hoped for, the evidence of things not seen.

Hebrews 11:1

God is inexplicable. He rests, having already created everything from nothing, yet He works with what He created. He dwells among us, His spirit made flesh in Jesus and now alive in us. He gives us choices, and we please Him by acknowledging His presence in our lives, even when things go wrong. Aware of the things we find overwhelming, He tells us not to worry.

Truly my soul silently *waits* for God; from Him *comes* my salvation. He only *is* my rock and my salvation; *He is* my defense; I shall not be greatly moved.

Psalm 62:1-2

His word contains the truth, uncensored and multidimensional, and represents our instructions for life.

He will be the sure foundation for your times, a rich store of salvation and wisdom and knowledge; the fear of the Lord is the key to this treasure.

Isaiah 33:6

Don't try to manage without using the instruction manual. Your Creator designed you for more than your current level of mastery. The Bible provides us with a direct connection to God's blessings. He knows that circumstances may not be ideal for us right now, but the love-language of scripture sends a message of hope for all people. Sovereign beyond my comprehension, He sets the stage. When we acknowledge His inspired plan for human relationships and learn our parts in the earthly drama, He provides exactly what we need in all circumstances.

"Is not my word like fire", declares the Lord, "and a hammer that breaks a rock in pieces?"

Jeremiah 23:29

One way or another, God will build a relationship with His people. The Word, throughout scripture, is synonymous with Jesus. We're on fire with His Spirit when we accept His invitation into the kingdom. The truth in God's word cracks open hardened hearts and stimulates spiritual growth. Then He instructs us as we go along. Internalize this concept of living as a child of God and imitate the character of our Father. His sovereign authority supersedes our interaction with Him, even as we think our own thoughts and choose our own actions.

"For My thoughts *are* not your thoughts, nor *are* your ways My ways," says the LORD. "For *as* the heavens are higher than the earth, so are My ways higher than your ways, and My thoughts than your thoughts."

Isaiah 55:8-9

At the very core of His personality we find His generous, perfect love poured out for all people, not just those who agree with you. Force your mind to align more closely with God's word and discover your identity as a child of your spiritual birth Father.

Sin

By jumping right into these Biblical texts, we learn to swim in the living waters.[6] It doesn't matter if we do a belly flop or a cannonball. Immersing ourselves in the truth, plunging deeper into our understanding of our own uncleanness, our willingness to submit to this purification process pleases God.

A believer needs to know what scripture tells us about our relationship with God, understanding that He wants us to seek good, not evil.[7] For the most part, people don't talk about sin anymore, even in church. Our definition of sin has grown fuzzy. So here we find one of the most troublesome repellent doctrines: **God set the standard of right and wrong**.

If we measure our sins by the harm done to others, we miss the mark and create our own values. Instead, we must consider the harm done to our relationship with God.

For everyone practicing evil hates the light and does not come to the light, lest his deeds should be exposed. But he who does

6   Revelation 7:17
7   Amos 5:14

the truth comes to the light, that his deeds may be clearly seen, that they have been done in God.

John 3:20-21

Sin damages our alliance with God and separates us from Him. However, He welcomes us back if we confess and repent.

For God did not send His Son into the world to condemn the world, but that the world through Him might be saved.

John 3:17

We see that God intends to bring us into His family. An earthly family abides by rules of conduct that reflect their values; our place in God's household mirrors this pattern. We need to know the spiritual ground rules to live as His children. When I looked up the root words for sin in the Hebrew language, I discovered the poignant use of the word *hatta't*. Hatta't implies the acknowledgement of sin and the reality of God's forgiveness, all wrapped up in the same word! It means both "sin" and "sin offering"[8]. Stop and think about that! Whether we missed the mark, deviated from God's standard, or ran away from God, He planted a seed of forgiveness in that sin. Then He waited for us to discover our error, confess, and turn back to Him.

We first need to acknowledge the sin in our lives. Satan's smoke and mirror techniques mesmerize the unsuspecting seeker with spiritual anesthesia. Trusting and unaware of the unaltered truth of the Bible, seekers fall for the idea that evil does not exist unless you believe in it. The notion that you can achieve a level of enlightenment, lifting yourself above the fray, leads to spiritual infidelity. This kind of wisdom lures people to see only the fundamental good in all men, leaving out the redemptive feature of God's grace in a fallen world. The latest trend to encompass all religions, to bind together in brotherly love, seems right on the surface. However, upon scrutiny, one does not find the truth negotiable. After all,

---

8   Encyclopedia of Bible Words by Lawrence O Richards, page 566

Satan himself believes in God[9], yet claims his own religion. Jesus came for all people, not for all religions. Here's what the Bible says about the inherent goodness of mankind:

As it is written: There is none righteous, no, not one; there is none who understands; there is none who seeks after God. They have all turned aside; they have together become unprofitable; there is none who does good, no, not one. Their throat is an open tomb; with their tongues they have practiced deceit; the poison of asps is under their lips; whose mouth is full of cursing and bitterness. Their feet are swift to shed blood; destruction and misery are in their ways; and the way of peace they have not known. There is no fear of God before their eyes.

Romans 3:10-18

God's love urges us to discern between good and evil and turn away from ungodliness. The first five books of the Bible, the Torah, spelled out God's instructions for the Israelites. It protected them from confusion over gray areas, clarifying what God considers detestable and what He calls "good". God set aside blessings for obedience and commanded specific punishments to be carried out for lawbreakers; the people should be holy and set apart from the "anything goes" cultures they encountered.

For before the law was given, sin was in the world. But sin is not taken into account when there is no law.

Romans 5:13

We hate to think about sin. We hesitate to mention it in a conversation. Yet without the law, we'd be oblivious to the mind of God, aside from our speculation or personal encounter with Him. God began to reveal His presence by spelling out His true nature and character to Adam. He dealt with Cain and Abel. The oral traditions, the stories of ancient men

---

9   James 2:19

walking and talking with God, paint a picture of what He loves and what He finds detestable. When God speaks to us personally, we confirm it by His word. In graphic detail, He lays out our choices: good and evil, life and death, blessings and curses, forgiveness and condemnation. If we love Him, we think about our response to His direct instructions. Paul uses this example:

For I would not have known covetousness unless the law had said, "You shall not covet."

Romans 7:7b

Why should we think about our sins and identify them?

For sin, taking occasion by the commandment, deceived me, and by it killed me.

Romans 7:11

We've grown accustomed to the idea that we'll die someday. But Paul wholeheartedly spells out the problem. When we face our sins by thinking about God's law, which ought to be a good thing to do, it creates a dilemma in our life. Our sins take over our flesh with uncanny ease, enslaving us to our carnal nature and separating us from God. Throughout history, people have followed the corruption of their fleshy desires, making a choice to refuse God.

The fool has said in his heart, "There is no God." They are corrupt, they have done abominable works, there is no one who does good. The LORD looks down from heaven upon the children of men, to see if there are any who understand, who seek God. They have all turned aside, they have together become corrupt; there is no one who does good, no, not one.

Psalm 14:1-3

Even so, the story of Jesus demonstrates God's compassion for everyone struggling with human frailties. Instead of waiting until we deserved God's grace, He submitted Himself to the unthinkable and opened a way for us to choose life with God.

For when we were still without strength, in due time Christ died for the ungodly. For scarcely for a righteous man will one die; yet perhaps for a good man someone would even dare to die. But God demonstrates His own love toward us, in that while we were still sinners, Christ died for us.

Romans 5:6-8

The Old Testament Laws reveal glimpses into the mind of God about our behavior and what He loves or hates. Instead of leaving us enslaved by our sinful nature, Jesus Christ bought and paid for us. We can choose to be a part of the eternal household of heaven. With that in mind, look in the book of James for a very practical view of sin:

Where do wars and fights *come* from among you? Do *they* not *come* from your *desires for* pleasure that war in your members? You lust and do not have. You murder and covet and cannot obtain. You fight and war. Yet you do not have because you do not ask. You ask and do not receive, because you ask amiss, that you may spend *it* on your pleasures. Adulterers and adulteresses! Do you not know that friendship with the world is enmity with God? Whoever therefore wants to be a friend of the world makes himself an enemy of God. Or do you think that the Scripture says in vain, "The Spirit who dwells in us yearns jealously"? But He gives more grace. Therefore He says: " *God resists the proud, but gives grace to the humble.*"

Therefore submit to God. Resist the devil and he will flee from you. Draw near to God and He will draw near to you. Cleanse *your* hands, *you* sinners; and purify *your* hearts, *you* double-minded. Lament and mourn and weep! Let your laughter be turned to mourning and *your* joy to gloom. Humble yourselves in the sight of the Lord, and He will lift you up.

Do not speak evil of one another, brethren. He who speaks evil of a brother and judges his brother, speaks evil of the law and judges the law. But if you judge the law, you are not a doer of the law but a judge. There is one Lawgiver, who is able to save and to destroy. Who are you to judge another?

Come now, you who say, "Today or tomorrow we will go to such and such a city, spend a year there, buy and sell, and make a profit"; whereas you do not know what *will happen* tomorrow. For what *is* your life? It is even a vapor that appears for a little time and then vanishes away. Instead you *ought* to say, "If the Lord wills, we shall live and do this or that." But now you boast in your arrogance. All such boasting is evil. Therefore, to him who knows to do good and does not do *it*, to him it is sin.

James 4

That pretty much categorizes us all as sinners. I wonder how many Christians breeze past that passage without a tear of remorse. The words make me want to wail out loud just to think of all the time I spent planning to carry on business and make money as if it held fulfillment. My heart weeps at the thought of those years when I judged the law and interpreted God's perfect principles through the prism of worldly lies.

Looking back I grieve that I misled souls with my double-mindedness as I pursued things of the world. When God's word reveals your error, remember *hatta't*. Jesus has already worked out your redemption. He's paid the price. Accept forgiveness and turn away from pride.

James wrote to Hebrew believers [10] who were very familiar with the word of God. He tells us that if we speak evil of our neighbor or spouse, God will not bless our relationships because we have alienated Him and judged His law. Alienating ourselves in any way from God is sin. Our skills in resisting the devil must be applied to every thought and word if we want to become children of God. When we exercise our spiritual senses by gaining knowledge of the law, we grow up and please our Father. Paul wrote:

---

10   Find the context, written to the twelve tribes scattered abroad, in James 1:1

For everyone who partakes only of milk is unskilled in the word of righteousness, for he is a babe. But solid food belongs to those who are of full age, that is, those who by reason of use have their senses exercised to discern both good and evil.

Hebrews 5:13-14

Pause and reflect on these words. Examine your own conscience. Stop and consider how they apply to you, allowing God's word to penetrate your heart as you listen for His voice. Let your tears flow and take a step closer to God, the One who knows you better than anyone. Make a commitment to exercise your senses to discern *both good and evil.*

Feel the sorrow of your mistakes and offer this to Him. Grieve as you think of how your selfish ways have taken you away from Him.[11] Think, really think, of how you searched for pleasure and came up wanting more. Know that God pursues you because your name remains in His book[12], and He calls you to fulfill His purpose, not yours.[13] Bring your problems and your pride to Him who already knows, and take a step toward the One who built His forgiveness into your sins. Then He will bring you close for comfort and instruction.

---

11   Lamentations 1:12-13
12   Revelations 21:27
13   Romans 8:28

THE TODAY TEXT

Drop your baggage if you hold onto the past. Forget all your plans for the future. We travel together on a journey into *Today*, with a capital T. When God instructed His writers to emphasize a specific word, I believe He intended for us to take a closer look at it.

> **Today, if you will hear His voice, do not harden your hearts as in the rebellion, in the day of trial in the wilderness, where your fathers tested Me, tried Me, and saw My works forty years. Therefore I was angry with that generation, and said, "They always go astray in their heart, and they have not known My ways." So I swore in My wrath, "They shall not enter My rest." Beware, brethren, lest there be in any of you an evil heart of unbelief in departing from the living God; but exhort one another daily, while it is called "Today," lest any of you be hardened through the deceitfulness of sin.**
>
> **Hebrews 3:7-13**

When I first began to meditate on chapters three and four in Hebrews, I thought, "God gives us a new chance to approach Him every day!" He kept calling me back to read it again and again, as if I missed something. It seemed as if He put the word *Today* in flashing neon lights, right over the Narrow Door of His Kingdom. He invites us to enter and learn about His mysteries while we live on this earth. Imagine that. He actually desires our company when we become **"partakers of the heavenly calling"**.[14]

Consider day seven after God completed His work and dedicated time for rest and enjoyment of His creation.[15] He had breathed out the vast universes with a word and set them in motion. To this day, creation groans and waits for the sons of God to be revealed[16]. Our opportunity to enter the Rest with Him, our day seven, starts *Today* when we pursue His ways. He put everything we need into motion in six days, and now waits for the proper time to gather us together for permanent earthly peace. As we practice for those eternal days ahead, God promises that we can enter the Rest with Him during tumultuous times. Imagine how frustrating He must find us when we make excuses and refuse to go in. Look closer with me at what I call the TODAY Text. Glimpse God's view of our hearts and attitudes.

> **For who, having heard, rebelled? Indeed, was it not all who came out of Egypt, led by Moses? Now with whom was He angry forty years? Was it not with those who sinned, whose corpses fell in the wilderness? And to whom did He swear that they would not enter His rest, but to those who did not obey? So we see that they could not enter in because of unbelief.**
>
> **Hebrews 3:16-19**

Did God watch over you in your spiritual desert when you strayed from Him? Ever since Adam and Eve, God has offered humankind the opportunity to trust Him for their every need. Do we live with the same lack of faith as those Hebrew travelers in the desert? Do we believe *in Him* while hanging onto distractions and fears, stopping at the edge of His promises? Obey Him by pushing those fears out of the way to follow Him.

---

14   Hebrews 3:1
15   Genesis 2:2
16   Romans 8:16-22

Therefore, since a promise remains of entering His rest, let us fear lest any of you seem to have come short of it. For indeed the gospel was preached to us as well as to them; but the word which they heard did not profit them, not being mixed with faith in those who heard *it.*

Hebrews 4:1-2

In our time, God still holds promises for us, and warns us against complaining when life seems hard.

Since therefore it remains that some *must* enter it, and those to whom it was first preached did not enter because of disobedience, again He designates a certain day, saying in David, *"Today,"* after such a long time, as it has been said: *"Today, if you will hear His voice, do not harden your hearts."*

Hebrews 4:6-7

We do not *enter the* R*est* by accident. It requires deliberate effort after our salvation, and indicates that we want to grow up in our faith.

There remains therefore a rest for the people of God. For he who has entered His rest has himself also ceased from his works as God *did* from His. Let us therefore be diligent to enter that rest, lest anyone fall according to the same example of disobedience.

Hebrews 4:9-11

God offers much more than a physical place and a day set aside for contemplating and worshiping Him. Jesus removed the veil. He wants us to abide in His presence all the time. TODAY. Why do we hesitate? Do we think we must be perfect to enter? Are we too busy right now? Do we even understand that He has extended an invitation to us?

Let's uncover a deeper significance of this Today text by reading about this Old Testament example, when Moses and the Israelites approached the Promised Land for the first time. Canaan represented their goal, their physical destination where they imagined life would finally be easy.

And the LORD spoke to Moses, saying, "Send men to spy out the land of Canaan, which I am giving to the children of Israel; from each tribe of their fathers you shall send a man, every one a leader among them."

Numbers 13:1-2

They sent out a group of trustworthy men to scout the land, finding grapes, figs, and pomegranates in the lush valleys. During their travels, however, they saw inhabitants much taller and stronger than any of them. By the time they returned to camp, they exaggerated the negative conditions they found in Canaan. Some of them probably predicted horror stories about getting squashed by the giants and being left for the buzzards. Can't you just hear them?

"We are not able to go up against the people, for they *are* stronger than we." And they gave the children of Israel a bad report of the land which they had spied out, saying, "The land through which we have gone as spies *is* a land that devours its inhabitants, and all the people whom we saw in it *are* men of *great* stature."

Numbers 13:31-32

All but two of the scouts shouted, "We seem like grasshoppers next to these people in Canaan. This is impossible. We don't want to die like that! We must turn back!" They took God out of the equation, blurted out their fearful words, and turned thousands of people away from the lush green hillsides and back into the desert.

Because of their lack of faith, God allowed them to *choose* strife in the wilderness instead of the blessings He planned for them. Listen carefully to His words to get a clue for Today about trusting Him in every difficult situation.

Because all these men who have seen My glory and the signs which I did in Egypt and in the wilderness, and have put Me to the test now these ten times, and have not heeded My voice,

47

they certainly shall not see the land of which I swore to their fathers, nor shall any of those who rejected Me see it.

Numbers 14:22-23

There, at the very crescendo of their journey, they found another obstacle. They refused to go the last mile when they arrived at their destination. They grumbled. They wept. They rebelled. They said it would be better to go back to Egypt and live as slaves. The faithless words of the scouts led to fear and began a chain reaction of doubting God. As badly as they needed a place to call home, they felt too tired to go further. The miracles God provided to sustain them along the way forgotten, their lack of faith influenced decisions that blocked them from their reward.

Thus says the LORD: "Stand in the ways and see, and ask for the old paths, where the good way *is, a*nd walk in it; Then you will find rest for your souls." But they said, "We will not walk *in it.*"

Jeremiah 6:16

More than ever before, people need to know the kind of peace that only comes with complete trust in God. With economic woes and destruction around the globe, we sense a paradigm shift approaching for our way of life. [17] Sin penetrates our culture so thoroughly that a person wonders if they could make any difference at all. We begin to feel like grasshoppers in the middle of sweeping winds of change. It's time to claim a courageous faith. Although God does not assure peace and security for our world, He promises that He will provide the strength necessary to overcome adversity.

Learning that His priorities differ from ours, we follow His precepts carefully until they become our way. Watch out though, for when you diligently obey Him, Satan will try to fill you up with pride about your spiritual development! The Pharisees ignored this problem. Many hard working religious folks fall into this category, thinking they are better than

---

17   Psalm 2:1-9

the next person because of their obedience. If you sense any sort of pride in your own thinking, stop and take hold of that spirit to throw it into the pit. We need to check for those sneaky little devils constantly. Religious arrogance hardened the hearts of the temple leaders during Jesus' time, and we see that same lack of love spilling over into our cultural differences.

Which do you think God approves of: the one who loudly objects to sinful behavior, or the one who extends His love and grace to the sinner? Thank goodness God judges our intent, for we often find ourselves fighting and debating about preserving the status quo in our society, when we need to listen for God's plan. The injustice that thwarts our freedom lures righteous people close to the spiritual quicksand. It's easy to get swept along in religious activism, placing national pride and fear of losing our comfortable lives over the mandate to love one another.

The real Promised Land is eternal; God requires absolute faith and unworldly courage. When we see God's interaction with us, and get a glimpse of the Promised Land, we certainly don't want to turn back in fear! If we remain habitually disobedient or feel too proud to change, we'll keep stumbling and cause others to fall by example.

YOUR TIME TO CHOOSE

The Today Text points to every hardship and says, "This is your time to make a choice." If you go along with the crowd or panic, then you cannot enter the Rest. In unsettling times we can take up a steady march toward righteousness. Filter out the negative chatter of the world and use words to build people up, focusing energy on God's purpose in His kingdom instead of self-preservation. When we think about our jobs, our homes, and our lives on earth, let's ask God what He thinks before we pray for more blessings. He'll point to our neighbors and give us enough to share. When we put Him back into the equation, we realize that He wrote the formula for our blessings!

Does God call us to go the extra mile in our personal relationships? Too discouraged to put forth the effort, we give in to the idea that friends, family and those in our faith community are expendable. God reconciles people when they choose to include Him. He protects us and shows us how to deal with tough situations so we might receive the promises of obedience. In all worthwhile endeavors, persistence and courage affect the outcome.

Following God together during an impossible challenge breaks through spiritual strongholds. He uses our greatest challenges to develop our divine skills. At every critical juncture in our lives we choose whether to seek God's guidance or to listen to the current wisdom and grumblings of the world.

If we pray, He requires obedient action. When we ignore Him, we enter into a sinful cycle of complaints, criticisms and, yes, seeking other gods. If we harbor an unrepentant spirit, we open ourselves to other spirits which bring us to our knees when they do their job. You might say that God uses them as learning tools to practice our faith. Obedience, on the other hand, requires faith to slip beyond the crowd gathered at the veil as we seek counsel with God Himself.

When the Messiah returns to remove our challenges and obstacles, He promises perfection and harmony for the world. Today, however, we occupy a sinful, broken terrain that snares and consumes us. As danger surrounds the globe, we're invited to develop unworldly skills by following the Way of our Savior. We belong together as one body, as a group of men, women, husbands, wives, families, communities of believers. We must function in groups because God expects us to edify and encourage one another as we sharpen our spiritual skills.

Nonetheless, in every crowd we get at least one complainer, one gossip, one person that prefers to find fault. You know, the one who tells you it's never been done that way, it's too hard or not worth the risk of heartache.

We all face difficult times together. If we turn back too soon without really trusting in God to come through, we miss the depth of our relationships that God envisions for us. If you want to enter the Promised Land of Today, don't give up or rely on your own power. During hard times this causes arguments and split-ups if pride hardens the heart. If we grumble, criticize, and wish we were someplace else, God allows us the freedom to wander in our own desert wasteland. We feel small and incapable, knowing that sin works into our daily life.

Today we have an opportunity to enter the Rest with a simple change of attitude. Where does our supply come from? Who sustains us and protects us? Do we possess the freedom to change our spiritual direction if we wander in the desert? Yes! *Today* speak words of faith. *Today* recognize your spiritual adversaries and defeat them because you believe God. Expect a difference in your life.

Are you overcome with debt? Recognize the power to change your attitude about it and overcome the old way of looking at it. Refuse the temptation to speak of it in any manner that does not improve it. Don't blame someone else and never complain about lack. Instead of saying, "We're broke." "Or we can't pay our bills." Say something like, "We're learning to be thrifty until our debts are paid, and God is meeting all of our needs!" or "We trust God to show us the way out of this situation." Then seek Him earnestly and do exactly what He tells you, no matter how ridiculous it seems or how long it takes. Start talking and thinking like a son of God. If you need to make a change, don't be too proud to obey His instructions.

Are you dealing with a serious illness or injury? Begin to think about it as if you're making an incredible discovery, where your physical comfort or lack of it seems less important while you spend this quiet time with God alone. Turn off the noise around you and seek Him. Call out to Him in your pain and He will draw near and reveal His character in you. He may force you to repent, especially if you thought *you* were in control. He may be doing a work in one of your family members, hospital staff, or co-workers, with you as the messenger. He may take you out of your routine to give you an indescribable gift of grace. I know from experience that God's children must think differently from everyone else if they want peace to come upon them during their trials.

Entering the Rest, we go into a spiritual courage filling-station. When we worship there in spirit and truth, He fuels us with uncompromising purpose. Physically, we appear no different than before, but the inner activity of spiritual peace overflows into our actions and words. His word plugs us into Him for a spiritual tune-up. The Today Text reminds us that we enter the Rest when we obey. Read God's word with an open heart, allowing it to judge and transform your mind and heart. The benefits are instant and impartial. God's word invites all people to experience the joy of His Spirit.

OPPORTUNITY IN AFFLICTION

When you focus only on your physical circumstances, you probably refuse to acknowledge His sovereignty in some area of your life. It's all you can do to keep everything going on your own. No matter how hard you work or how perfect you try to be, an underlying problem always seems to be lurking just below the surface of life. When you surrender everything, you become a member of God's household, protected and blessed because you love Him with all your heart and all your soul. [18] He does not guarantee a trouble-free existence, but gives purpose to your growing pains.

You submit to discipline and He refines your disposition as you mature in faith. Then your circumstances hold no power over you. Where you once found frustration, you now see opportunities to help. You look at your enemies through new eyes of love. Instead of questioning your own sense of worth, you now understand that God created you with the unique ability to accomplish His specific purpose during your time on earth. No one else can replace you. No one else has walked in your shoes.

God knows when you honestly change directions, mentally turning away from your sin. He draws you near to come clean spiritually and

---

18   Deuteronomy 30:6

53

admit that you have a problem. He counts this as obedience, a first step. The physical impossibility overwhelms you when you actually try to stop sinning, and you would soon start back down the same path of destruction if not for Jesus. His Spirit empowers you to do the hardest part.

If you thought you needed a strong faith to prove yourself before God, realize that's backwards from the spiritual reality. Just turn to Him and He'll be your strength. Be watchful, for God uses special tools during these times in our lives, hardening hearts, turning up the heat, letting us fall, and sometimes allowing our problems to worsen so we won't procrastinate about faith any longer. Sometimes hitting bottom is the only way that you can start over. Consider it an opportunity.

Everyone comes to that place. One man may lose everything he owns before he humbles himself before God. Someone else struggles with addiction for years before finally hitting bottom hard enough to change directions and follow Christ. People agonize over broken relationships; others deal with disease, bitterness or loneliness, and many live under the weight of generational sins. Debt, death, pain, divorce and destructive habits all have one thing in common: the potential to bring us to our knees. We hope God created us for better things, but we must learn to handle the messy details of the flesh with a sense of grace and humor while "it is still Today".

I hope you look back on the worst days of your life to see the marker that says "Turning Point", the place where God changed you. All of your previous shameful deeds erased, He makes all things new. He waits for you to choose your time. He understands the depth of your sorrows and wants to heal those wounds. There is no shame in hitting the low spot; there is great sorrow in staying there. Begin to identify this circumstance and find the words to tell about it. Then simply follow His Way. Change your vocabulary to reflect the honorable character of a son or daughter of the Most High God. Tell about the obedience that prompted God to mend your life and change all the rest of your Todays.

Few of us would ever seek Him earnestly if we did not *need* Him. You'll see that God imbedded this important aspect of our faith into His plan.

Teach me good judgment and knowledge, for I believe Your commandments. Before I was afflicted I went astray, but now I keep Your word.

Psalm 119:66-67

We need a *before and after* in our lives. Before I was afflicted, I lived such a good life. I believed in an amazing and loving God. I thought I had everything a person could want. But when I was recovering from my fall, I carefully searched His word for something deeper. I recognized the signal. The disruption in my life was a blessing from my Heavenly Father who wanted to spend some private time with me. Now I'm beginning to see His interaction with me more clearly when things happen. I've learned to fine-tune my relationship with God when He communicates through circumstances. I want to follow Him wholeheartedly. Instead of feeling unlucky when something goes wrong, I know that it works for the good because I love Him.

We'd like to think God will soothe our hurts and fix our problems so we can go on our merry way. Sometimes we wonder why He overlooked us and left us desolate and struggling to cope with our troubles. Notice the self-serving slant on such thinking. If you want to go into the kingdom to learn from your Father, focus on what *He wants* next time you have a problem. He wants us to seek Him, obey Him, and learn His ways. He wants us to grow up to recognize and overcome the adversaries of His kingdom, and then teach others who go astray.

God expects regular attitude adjustments among His children, or they must repeat their lessons collectively again and again. True healing in all relationships starts with an uncomfortable change in both thinking and behavior. Oh, the pain of letting go of what we thought we wanted! Oh, the disappointment we experience when we realize that we don't exist for our own self-satisfaction! We're shocked to find out that we came all this way, exhausted and worn, just to encounter the biggest challenge ever! We all end up in places just like that at some point in our lives.

My soul faints for Your salvation, but I hope in Your word. My eyes fail from searching Your word, saying, "When will You comfort me?"

Psalm 119:81-82

The Holy Spirit brings comfort in due time, but we simply do not exist for our own comfort and enjoyment. God's sovereign authority to deal with us through our sorrows makes us wonder about the whole process.

Direct my steps by Your word, and let no iniquity have dominion over me.

Psalm 119:133

Look up the Hebrew word **iniquity: "aven[19], from an unused root, perhaps meaning properly, to pant (hence, to exert oneself, usually in vain); trouble, wickedness, sorrow, idolatry."**
When you feel like you're constantly dealing with troubles, God plans to use them for your growth. He does not expect you to get bogged down in them, but rather to overcome, knowing that He holds the power of your victory. If your life seems difficult right now, keep pursuing your relationship with God. Your problems may stem from spending your energy on vain and self-centered desires. If these things lead to regret, then you know your name is in the Book of Life. He's drawing you into the kingdom to learn something important. He wants you to stand out in the crowd as one who walks in peace and praises God for His glory. Ask Him for advice and learn to conquer the demons of the flesh that try to steal your days. Look at the spiritual, not the physical.

My son, do not despise the chastening of the LORD, nor detest His correction; for whom the LORD loves He corrects, just as a father the son *in whom* he delights.

Proverbs 3:11-12

---

19   Strong's H5771, Condensed Brown-Driver-Briggs Hebrew Lexicon, Thayer's Greek Lexicon

Despite all our shortcomings, relapses into disobedience, and failures, God has not given up on us. He arranged a doorway into His kingdom for us while we live on earth. We may feel too weak to go in there alone. Jesus holds out a nail pierced hand, ready to lead us into the Rest. The spirit of pride may try to stop you, so prepare for battle against it. Use the word of God to build an arsenal against such enemies.

Reading his book of Psalms, you see that David's warrior prowess grew out of absolute faith that God wins. He practiced alone as a boy defending his father's sheep. Later in life, he fought his own spirit of pride and his tendency toward selfish desires. When he sinned and stumbled, his anguish led him into a much closer relationship with God. He loved God's laws and followed them to become a powerful leader.

Oh, how I love your law! It is my meditation all the day. You, through Your commandments, made me wiser than my enemies; for they are ever with me. I have more understanding than all my teachers, for Your testimonies are my meditation. I understand more than the ancients, because I keep Your precepts. I have restrained my feet from every evil way, that I may keep Your word.

Psalm 119:97-101

Our adversaries are ever with us. We wake up every day with demons crouching, poised to jump in with a terrible attitude or a fearful thought. Things can go from bad to worse if we do not listen to our Father's instructions. He placed them in the kingdom for a purpose, so don't make too much of them or they will try to take over your life. They pose no threat unless you give them a place. Our love for the things of the flesh may cause us to avoid keeping His precepts. We may feel angry with Him for allowing things to turn out the way they have so far. Or, we may think He wouldn't want anything to do with us while we continue to sin.

Jesus meets us with open arms of love in that very moment we call out to Him. He is the advocate, not the accuser. He encourages us to see the truth, acknowledge our faults, accept His forgiveness and then get about the family business.

Let my soul live, and it shall praise You; and let Your judgments help me. I have gone astray like a lost sheep; seek Your servant, for I do not forget Your commandments.
Psalm 119:175-176

We tend to think of judgment as a punishment for our error, but look at it another way. Have you considered how God's judgment can help your situation? Begin to understand that God placed His law as a framework for peace and excellence in your life. He gave these laws to His chosen people. They do not belong to everyone, but He extends them to those who choose to join His family. We live under the protection of His power when we love His laws and try to imagine how His words became our world. By submitting to righteous *judgment*, we gain authority in the spiritual kingdom, grow in faith by *learn* from our mistakes. It's a humbling experience, but an integral part of our spiritual walk.

WHEN SATAN TURNS UP THE HEAT

If we think we're ok on our own, then He may allow the enemy to increase the pressure, and then see if that makes a difference. If He's preparing us for something, He may send an adversary to give us specialized exercise and practice. [20] God does not promise a painless way of life, but uses each problem on earth to develop our spiritual character. When we're reborn of the spiritual family, we must continue to pursue the knowledge of God's kingdom and use our authority over the devil. Instead of ignoring the devil because we cannot see him, we gain awareness about overcoming this opponent. We continue to make mistakes, receive correction and grow up as we get better at recognizing our enemy.

See how your purpose comes to light when your heartfelt emotions pour out to God:

---

20   Read Job 1:8-12 to see that the LORD pointed out Job to Satan and then gave him permission to test him.

Hear my cry, O God; attend to my prayer. From the end of the earth I will cry to You, when my heart is overwhelmed; lead me to the rock that is higher than I. For You have been a shelter for me, a strong tower from the enemy. I will abide in Your tabernacle forever; I will trust in the shelter of Your wings. For You, O God, have heard my vows; You have given me the heritage of those who fear Your name.

Psalm 61:1-5

Satan will do anything to distract us from recognizing the sovereignty of God. The adversary reminds us of our shame and lures us into complaints and excuses. He pools our guilt and encourages us to wallow in it. If we get past these tricks, then he offers a tainted "spirituality" that keeps us thinking that we cannot, or need not, change. He deceives us with his lure of comfort and conformity.

"I'm not a bad person."

"I haven't really sinned."

That's the lie we need to overcome. We all miss the mark in some way, and God made allowances for it. Satan tells us we can achieve and perfect our own spiritual power with nothing more than self-control. But each time we come to a dead end in life, God gives us a chance to turn away from this kind of thinking.

If our sorrow leads to repentance, God turns it into a life-saving event we cannot fully comprehend.

Godly sorrow produces repentance leading to salvation and leaves no regret, but worldly sorrow brings death.

2 Corinthians 7:10

Every painful event in our life is orchestrated in the spiritual kingdom to give us an opportunity to stop and turn to God. Sometimes we flounder in misery. Other times we resolve to do better on our own power. Both lead to death. Whether I forge ahead with a disobedient spirit, or protest about unlucky circumstances and unrighteous actions of others, I perpetuate the deadly cycle I hate.

When I choose to approach God with a willingness to change, His mercy comforts me and I pass a little spiritual test. However, when I learn to defeat my inner adversaries by God's strength alone, I declare the works of the Lord and His mighty power to change everything.

> **You pushed me violently, that I might fall, but the LORD helped me. The LORD is my strength and song, and He has become my salvation. ... I shall not die, but live, and declare the works of the LORD. The LORD has chastened me severely, but He has not given me over to death. Open to me the gates of righteousness; I will go through them, and I will praise the LORD.**
>
> **Psalm 118:13-19**

Jesus shed His blood to remove our fault; we can surrender our old ways of thinking and lay them at the altar of God[21]. He burns them up. Imagine them going up in smoke, a fragrant aroma to God as we watch them disappear forever[22].

Contemplate the sacrifice Christ made, the pain and humiliation He endured for mankind. Understand that He will never leave us alone. He let them pierce His body, torture and scorn Him, just to make it possible for us to spend eternity with Him. Talk about a relationship! What love! What compassion! What mercy! That is the kind of love we want. That is the kind of love we were made for, both here on earth and in heaven.

---

21   Psalm 188:22-28
22   Hebrews 9:11-14

HUNGRY FOR THE TRUTH

Until we get our relationship right with God, we cannot rest, not even a little. Life, no matter how full, will be meaningless; our yearning for spiritual depth drives us to keep searching for Him. Jesus' sacrifice gives us direct access to God when we believe in Him, *confess* our shortcomings, and *obey*. Many of us have perfected the believing and confessing part, but distaste for obedience keeps us from a wholesome connection with God. Habitual sin becomes a stumbling block.

> **Ho! Everyone who thirsts, come to the waters; and you who have no money, come, buy and eat. Yes, come, buy wine and milk without money and without price. Why do you spend money for *what is* not bread, and your wages for *what* does not satisfy? Listen carefully to Me, and eat *what is* good, and let your soul delight itself in abundance.**
>
> **Isaiah 55:1-2**

Jesus, the author of our faith,[23] knows that spiritual matters seem elusive to humans. With infinite patience He teaches and revises us until

---

23   Hebrews 12:12

we get into the Rest with Him. The mysterious connection that draws a man to his Creator grows into a lifelong relationship. He offers us the spiritual food we crave as we open our hearts and minds and regularly consume God's word. Sometimes you need to savor one delicacy, a precept that God directly speaks to your heart. Other days, you need to fill yourself to overflowing with His words of confidence, seeking His will. The more of God's word you consume, the more you care about other people with an eternal perspective. You learn that you get back what you give.

And remember the words of the Lord Jesus, that He said, "It is more blessed to give than to receive."

Acts 20:35b

As we love God, likewise He pours His love through us onto others. It is more of surrender than of action at first. But as we get into the hearty solid food stage of our Christian adolescence, the pages of the Bible come alive as we digest them. They expand us as we become part of the story. We learn to hear God's voice when we spend time with Him. His words move us into action, but instead of our own selfish direction, we follow Jesus. He fills us with satisfaction and blesses our hunger for righteousness.

Blessed *are* the undefiled in the way, who walk in the law of the LORD! Blessed *are* those who keep His testimonies, who seek Him with the whole heart! They also do no iniquity; they walk in His ways. You have commanded *us t*o keep Your precepts diligently. Oh, that my ways were directed to keep Your statutes! Then I would not be ashamed, when I look into all Your commandments. I will praise You with uprightness of heart, when I learn Your righteous judgments. I will keep Your statutes; oh, do not forsake me utterly! How can a young man cleanse his way? By taking heed according to Your word. With my whole heart I have sought You; oh, let me not wander from Your commandments! Your word I have hidden in my heart, that I might not sin against You. Blessed *are* You, O LORD!

Teach me Your statutes. With my lips I have declared all the judgments of Your mouth. I have rejoiced in the way of Your testimonies, as *much as* in all riches. I will meditate on Your precepts, and contemplate Your ways. I will delight myself in Your statutes; I will not forget Your word. Deal bountifully with Your servant, that I may live and keep Your word. Open my eyes, that I may see wondrous things from Your law. I *am* a stranger in the earth; do not hide Your commandments from me. My soul breaks with longing for Your judgments at all times.

Psalm 119:5-20

The psalmist identified the error of his ways by familiarizing himself with God's laws and commands. He praised God as he confessed his imperfection and willingness to change. He craved a relationship with God, recognized his ties with heaven, and felt like a stranger on earth. Read this prayer often and hide the words in your heart. Develop a thirst for the righteousness of God. Experience the surge of the Almighty Creator stirring in you. The recipe for true spiritual power combines faith and obedience. Your soul craves God's wonder to be revealed in His law. Jesus said:

If you keep My commandments, you will abide in My love, just as I have kept My Father's commandments and abide in His love.

John 15:10

As our civilization prospers in the 21st century, we experience a constant barrage of ideas from which to choose as we celebrate diversity. With the world increasing in knowledge, basic truths fall prey to the popular culture. Often we're distracted with good intentions, trying to keep our bodies healthy as we neglect our spirit.

Do not be carried about with various and strange doctrines. For *it is* good that the heart be established by grace, not with foods which have not profited those who have been occupied with them.

Hebrews 13:9-10

We replace our hunger for self-satisfaction with a soul-filling banquet when we follow the way of Christ. Strangers on earth, we possess a spiritual hunger, a vacuum satisfied by God alone. Satan offers seeds of disobedience as he tempts with his tainted logic. He lures people into thinking they can snack on spiritual knowledge by listening to each other instead of God. Diluting our faith to make it easier to swallow and more socially acceptable in a diverse culture, we put ourselves in grave danger. It seems like a small omission, but cuts out countless huge blessings.

In the book of Revelation, we learn that everyone will be judged according to their works when the Book of Life is opened. [24] God will hold us accountable for every word we speak, (and if I know God, every thought we think). Then He will wipe away every tear. No more death or sorrow or pain. Death and Hades will be cast into the lake of fire, a black hole where they simply cease to be.

I will give of the fountain of the water of life freely to him who thirsts. He who overcomes shall inherit all things, and I will be his God and he shall be My son. But the cowardly, unbelieving, abominable, murderers, sexually immoral, sorcerers, idolaters, and all liars shall have their part in the lake which burns with fire and brimstone, which is the second death.

Revelation 21:6b-8

We need to check ourselves and make sure that our actions reveal spiritual courage and faith. If we're simply drifting along comfortably, then how thirsty will we be? If we're completely at ease, then why would

---

24   Revelation 20:13

64

we need courage? The mystery of God's word cannot reveal itself to anyone unless they seek it with faith. Sharpen your skill in the knowledge of scripture; seek wise, loving teachers, testing everything for the truth in the Bible by the Holy Spirit. When you listen, and God gives you an assignment, do it immediately. It will require courage, but you'll find yourself farther and farther away from the old fleshy desires and fears that once shackled you.

TOXIC DISTRACTIONS

All of us live with exposure to toxic distractions of the flesh. Our children live amid horrendous offenses and abominations to God, their hearts and minds being influenced by violence and mediocrity. The age of innocence seems lost in a brew of destructive yeast that threatens our families. We feel the pressure of daily demands and expectations.

In an effort to deal with (or escape) the enormous stress, people take drugs to alter their speed. Doctors and experts recommend it. *If you can't slow your mind enough to sleep, take a pill to fix it, they say. If you can't control your temper, the pharmaceutical companies have multiple remedies. If you can't get up the courage or energy to do all that this world demands, try a different prescription or go for therapy. If you can't stand the pain, just buffer it with a pill. If you find yourself depressed, get a prescription for happiness.* I'm not saying these things are wrong, but we must recognize them as distractions that keep us too weak to learn the family business. The more we buy into such "wisdom", the more we think about ourselves and how we feel. The sorceries of our age, drugs of all descriptions, legal and illegal, represent billions of dollars. They have become such a means of commerce in our world that the masses bow down to serve these idols and find themselves enslaved to them.

Pharmaceutical drugs lay claim to the psychological and physical well-being of an expanding group of vulnerable people. With all of the wonderful medical and scientific advances, our people perish from a lack of knowledge of God. [25] Satan suppresses our ability to apply knowledge of

---

25   Hosea 4:6

spiritual health with pseudo-intellectual arguments against it. We live in a time when the wonders of science could recover our vitality if we combined its applications with God's wisdom. But for the most part, people feel too drained just getting through their physical day to pursue their spiritual life. While we strive to improve (or maintain) our circumstances, we miss the joy of life in the spirit.

Some people try stimulants and suppressants such as caffeine and alcohol. Others try to eat and drink the most wholesome and pure foods they can find. If that doesn't make them feel good about themselves, they may need a weekend seminar, complete with tapes and books, to reprogram for success. We humans get so wrapped up in the physical successes, that we sometimes forget the spiritual kingdom entirely. That's exactly what Satan wants[26].

The world says you're either too fat or too skinny, and you should change that by altering your lifestyle. You have plenty of money or not enough, and either way, your purchases don't satisfy for long. You may stand ready to defend your faith with words, but, dashing out to all of the important activities, you may not even have time to know your next door neighbor. You want a perfect family, and that seems almost attainable on a good day, so you think you're on the right path, and think it worth the pressure. Our grand ideas of worldly accomplishments, however noble and right, lead our families dangerously close to the quicksand.

Jesus taught us to listen to Him and respond with action.

But everyone who hears these sayings of Mine, and does not do them, will be like a foolish man who built his house on the sand...

Matthew 7:26

Slow down and look at the groundwork of your spiritual house. Ask God to reveal His purpose in your life. Invite Him into your home with your heart prepared for obedience. Then remember that obedience begins in the mind. If you want peace in your home, accept it now.

---

26   Proverbs 23:19-21

Now may the Lord of peace Himself give you peace always in every way.

2 Thessalonians 3:16a

Memorize this. Imagine and believe that He offers you **"peace-always in every way."** Understand the difference between peace on earth and spiritual peace. When we hunger for that inner satisfaction of knowing God and then try to pursue it by methods and formulas, it takes on the shape of a mental exercise. There we go again, striving for spiritual fitness so we can climb our way to heaven. That's idolatry.

Instead of tantalizing our taste buds with appetizers until we get to heaven, Jesus invites us into the garden with Him to satisfy our soul with the succulent fruits of a peace-filled spirit. There He teaches us to use the power and authority that rightfully belong to the heirs of His kingdom. We eat the muscle building spiritual meat of His mystery.

Our society warps our perception and creates a multitude of what I call "reality disorders". For example, people with eating disorders suffer first in their minds because our world places so much emphasis on the outward appearance. With a sense of reality distorted by immersion in worldly culture, their heart begins to break as they try to alter physical appearances. The world blames it on their sense of self-worth. The world offers temporary cures by teaching proper diet habits and methods to improve self-esteem.

In the same way, people strive to live up to the world's vision of happiness and success and wind up feeling depressed and unworthy. As we age, we attempt to repair our bodies, trying to look and feel our best, knowing all the while that our flesh progresses toward death. We seek one quick fix after another for our ailments and shortcomings. This distracts us from our spiritual destiny.

In contrast, the purifying baptism of repentance and receiving Jesus' healing Spirit represents immersion into a different culture than the world offers. Real worth starts in the spirit, far removed from the cults of self-worship and/or self-loathing. True believers possess the promise of rebirth and new beginnings. They have exchanged their old life for a vital, timeless recognition of their true identity. Living in the kingdom of God, you learn to recognize good and evil, and **rely upon the spiritual appearance as the true reality**. Worldly logic finds this repellent, but you verify the truth of your spirit as you live life.

The more you think about yourself, the more difficult you'll find it to live up to the standards and expectations imposed by the world. If you want to participate in the feast of His kingdom, go to Jesus just as you are now and tell Him you want to live in His presence. He won't ask you to do a lot of preparation. [27] He'll refine you with His Spirit of fire and then cleanse you with His living water. He will melt away the pounds of heavy self-concern and wash away the contaminants. He wants to reveal His love to you in an intimate way that cannot be described. Yes, you.

He wants His loved ones to feel fully satisfied, always rested, and always ready to work in the kingdom. Believers move out of spiritual lethargy when they detoxify and renew their minds. They know they can enter the Rest any time they please, but often hang onto something old and familiar instead. Like children refusing to eat their spiritual vegetables, they reject the manna from heaven and seek the secular junk food of this world. They don't understand what they lack, but keep asking the same question: "Is this enough, Lord?"

Get an exhilarating spiritual makeover, replenishing the soul and then literally making each cell new. When you ingest that small seed of faith and begin to nurture it, you take on a radiant glow that heals others as well as yourself.

Beloved, now we are children of God: and it has not yet been revealed what we shall be, but we know that when He is revealed, we shall be like Him, for we shall see Him as He is. And everyone who has this hope in Him purifies himself, just as He is pure.

1 John 3:2-3

---

27   Mark 2:11

Jesus calls us into the kingdom for purification and teaches us, His brothers and sisters, the Way. Listen to Him. You may hear him saying, "Let go of yourself and allow my Spirit to fill the temple within you. Let me purify your tabernacle and teach you how to keep it pure. As you seek my wisdom and crave my words, they will satisfy and give you strength."

He reminds us, "You need to travel light." We begin to let go of our own ideas of perfection. He continues. "Take nothing for yourself." This is where we begin to negotiate. Surely He speaks figuratively. "Nothing," He repeats. Do this and it will transform your life and everyone around you. Forget about yourself and you will be shaped perfectly to enter the narrow door of the Rest.

CHOOSING THE WAY

When Paul stood before the governor, being accused by his fellow
Jews of crimes, he explained that he worshipped in the Jewish
temple as a follower of the Way.

> **And they neither found me in the temple disputing with anyone
> nor inciting the crowd, either in the synagogues or in the city.
> Nor can they prove the things of which they now accuse me.
> But this I confess to you, that according to the Way which they
> call a sect, so I worship the God of my fathers, believing all
> things which are written in the Law and in the Prophets.**
>
> **Acts 24:12-14**

When Paul described the Way, explaining that the Messiah had been
crucified and resurrected, the religious leaders labeled his new way of life a
sect! The early New Testament church went to the Temple and synagogues
to read God's word together. Many Jews and Gentiles believed in Jesus
as the Messiah and followed the Way. Disappointed but not surprised
when some of his own people rejected Him, he continued to explain the
fulfillment of the prophecies through Christ.

**I have hope in God ... that there will be a resurrection of the
dead, both of the just and the unjust. This being so, I myself
always strive to have a conscience without offense toward God
and men.**

Acts 24:15-16

Paul confessed that he worked hard all of his life to keep his conscience
clear before God and men. However, he'd found a very real way to walk in
power using the righteous discernment of Christ's Spirit.

The idea of "striving toward righteousness" sounds like a painful
exercise against fleshy desires. I get a picture of endless swimming
against a river current in my mind. Living on a river with a swift current, I
know you cannot keep that up for long. It's exhausting and unsustainable,
providing a brief cardio and muscular workout. Each time you try it, you
last a little longer. God did not intend for us to fight against our flesh
all the time; I know that He created us for something more and gave us
His Spirit to help us get into the flow of the kingdom. However, we need
to exercise our faith regularly, resisting the power of the flesh, getting
past the struggle all the way to the peaceful flow. It's dangerous, wild and
breathtaking to cooperate with God's Spirit in this way.

I wonder, if Paul, with his great faith and knowledge, strived to keep
his conscience clear, what of the rest of us? For the answer, I found it
helpful to look closer at what it means to "strive". From the Greek verb,
"askeo[28] translates: **to form by art, to adorn OR to exercise (one's) self,
take pains, labor, strive."**

We all need to deal with our own worries, doubts or weaknesses,
striving to pull away from the sin in our life. We do not fight each other, but
the evil inclination within us. Meanwhile, God wants us to know that He's
forming us into something beautiful and useful. Our participation makes
a difference in the outcome, both for ourselves and the world around us.
God expects us to overcome sinful tendencies on earth, each according
to our ability. Our cooperation with the Creator essential, *we determine*
whether we're honed as a fine instrument or struggle against His hand.

---

28   Strong's G778, Condensed Brown-Driver-Briggs Hebrew Lexicon, Thayer's Greek Lexicon

Throughout scripture we find that God forms us with great patience and care. He forges us in the fire[29] or molds us like clay.[30] He edits the pages of our lives[31] and polishes our faith. Our consciences conform to the shape of divine art, and righteous actions adorn us when we choose the Way. Instead of struggle, we find grace. Instead of conflict, we see order in the making.

> **For by grace you have been saved through faith, and that not of yourselves; it is the gift of God, not of works, lest anyone should boast. For we are His workmanship, created in Christ Jesus for good works, which God prepared beforehand that we should walk in them.**
>
> **Ephesians 2:8-10**

From our viewpoint, as the creation, it seems awkward and sometimes painful. We feel we've been put through the fire as our Maker fashions our character to be more like Him. Occasionally we break down,[32] and often we worry too much about ourselves. If only we could grasp this concept of our spiritual formation, we might cooperate more fully. But sadly, we tend to spend most of our time pointing out the sins of our loved ones and enemies rather than struggling against the flesh, fighting our own bad attitudes and weaknesses.

We know that God blesses men who struggle with their faith and come out on the other side with an obedient spirit. He gave Jacob a new name when He wrestled with the Angel of the LORD. Jonah ran from God and did not stop until the whale swallowed him, but when he followed God's instructions, many Gentiles turned to righteousness. David agonized over his disobedience, ultimately allowing God to forge him into a stronger vessel that poured out volumes of righteous wisdom and praise. If not for the resistance, life would be mundane. When we're brought to our own sacred struggles, God hopes that we discern the real battle within, and

---

29   Malachi 3:3
30   Isaiah 64:8
31   Hebrews 12:2
32   Psalm 51:17-18

overcome the spirits that try to keep us down.

Sometimes believers settle into a respectful but lifeless faith until they grasp the meaning behind these words. If you find yourself among them, fall out of the ranks of the lukewarm and find out what God expects you to overcome by the power of His Spirit. He designed each one of us for some unique reason in mind. We find joy in the pursuit of this purpose, but rarely do we find purpose in the pursuit of happiness.[33] I hope this makes you uncomfortable. I hope it makes you aware of the next thing you must overcome, so that your victory points to the glory of God.

I feel a special burden to understand the fight against addictions and overcoming the power of the flesh. Digging a little deeper, I looked up the root word for "askeo", (strive or exercise). God began to show me something new about seeking spiritual transformation. **"Skeuos:[34] a vessel, an implement...household utensils ...the tackle of armament of vessels... and metaphorically, a man of quality, a chosen instrument OR in a bad sense, an assistant in accomplishing an evil deed."** It is interesting to note that the term vessel was a common Greek metaphor for body, since Greeks thought of souls as living temporarily in bodies.

God gives us, His creations, choice in the way we turn out. I find that astonishing each time He reveals it to me! This reoccurring thread in the Bible gives us a glimpse into the nature of eternal life. We have the opportunity to participate in our own transformation into quality instruments for His purpose. Each day we adorn our bodies with the beauty of useful works in His kingdom.

When I'm rough around the edges, I submit to Him while He shows me how to chisel properly. From our perspective, we feel like we are striving against our natural inclinations. But God's idea puts something much more profound into motion when we allow His Spirit to take over our flesh. He's never wasteful, taking special notice of the lost and demoralized among us. How often He uses our brokenness to help another when we allow Him to interact with us!

---

33   wonderful saying from Monty Sholund in a lecture from Village Schools of the Bible
34   Strong's G4632, Condensed Brown-Driver-Briggs Hebrew Lexicon, Thayer's Greek Lexicon

I hope these words pique your interest to search this out and look at some of Paul's toughest repellent teachings about **overcoming the flesh.** Discover how to go beyond earthly strife to serve as a finely crafted **vessel** in the king's **armada.** See the worlds beyond. We literally need to **take pains** to shape our new identity, until we break free of our worldly ideas and resolve wholeheartedly to serve. With such commitment, we find satisfaction and reward.

A sense of right and wrong enables a person to choose between spiritual (God) and physical (man) priorities, while living in both worlds. It triggers the need to seek God here and now and try to see where we stand with Him.

In Athens, Paul told the philosophers that they were very religious when he saw an altar for the UNKNOWN GOD among their pagan objects of worship.

Therefore the One whom you worship without knowing Him, I proclaim to you: God, who made the world and everything in it, since He is Lord of heaven and earth, does not dwell in temples made with hands, nor is He worshiped with men's hands, as though He needed anything, since He gives to all life, breath, and all things.

Acts 17:23-25

Spiritual creatures in human vessels, we wonder how and why God created us. Yet a growing population says "there is no God" and "no one created us". This idea carves away at a long-held paradigm, for we know that even the Greeks thought of the body as a container for the soul. When you look back at cultures in ancient history, most people believed that some sort of god existed when they debated about *who He was*. In these times, some people find it more logical to take responsibility for their own life than to worship and follow an invisible being.

Those who choose not to delve into these mysteries carefully may fall prey to vain deceptions instead of sound reasoning. Such logic moves our thinking away from the real discussion about overcoming in the spirit. If you refuse to take a stand, I assure you that by default your vessel may be taken over for evil purposes.

Fulfillment of our true purpose hinges on our willingness to receive the spirit of wisdom and revelation in the knowledge of God. We outsmart the devil by taking on the greatness of God's power,[35] but such power does not always come upon us suddenly and without effort. We need to prove ourselves dedicated and reliable in the kingdom of God. That seems obvious to me, but human nature lures us toward instant gratification. We want to feel good about ourselves, and our spiritual commitment comes in fits and starts. Instead of submitting our life to become a work of art by the Creator Himself, we so easily follow our feelings most of the time. God patiently gives us another Today and smiles as He polishes us with loving hands.

Loving us as He does, He sent the Spirit of His Son to teach, encourage, and comfort us as we realize His plan for our lives. Rather than giving one great purpose to each of us, He's made provisions for our practice. When we overcome the demons of the flesh by winning in these spiritual tests, we train for a greater purpose. The purpose is not to live a glorious life on earth, but to bring others into God's presence by pointing out the Way into the kingdom. In this process of sanctification, we grow close to God as we glorify Him. He's oblivious to our past sins, freeing us to move forward with confidence. When we accept this truth, we open ourselves up to the majesty of His generosity.[36]

The simple faith of a Spirit-filled child of God hushes all debate about who is greater or wiser. Humble sons of God choose to become servants. Helping those who need to see the love of God, their actions lead them into a powerful peace that transcends the chaos of our times. This is the Way of Christ, open for all.

Believers place their hope in the resurrection of the dead. They'll get to heaven when they die, but how much effort goes into learning the spiritual Way, here and now? The church comes alive as the body of Christ when

35 Ephesians 1:17-19
36 Psalm 103:11-12

people overcome their pride and go out from their comfortable places to live as useful utensils for God. Walk the walk and speak the truth. In these times, people of faith need to know they are not finished yet!

Strengthen the weak hands, and make firm the feeble knees. Say to those who are fearful hearted, "Be strong, do not fear! Behold, your God will come with vengeance, with the recompense of God; He will come and save you."... A highway shall be there, and a road, and it shall be called the Highway of Holiness. The unclean shall not pass over it, but it shall be for others. Whoever walks the road, although a fool, shall not go astray.

Isaiah 35:3-8

SPIRITUALLY MINDED

G od designed the spirit world to function under His authority. Jesus came to show us the Way in. He prayed "on earth as it is in heaven"[37], revealing that our activity on earth *reflects* our movement in heaven. When Satan takes a stronghold, the resulting hatred, depression or tragedy appears rock-solid in someone's life. However, when the love of Christ starts a spiritual transformation, that same hopeless person discovers joy. The weary and lost find rest even though their physical circumstances remain the same. The lonely turn to their Father and find a relationship that's real. The abused and injured find a God who heals so completely that they literally begin to change in their flesh. Paul tried to explain that it begins in the mind:

> **For those who live according to the flesh set their minds on the things of the flesh, but those *who live* according to the Spirit, the things of the Spirit. For to be carnally minded *is* death, but to be spiritually minded *is* life and peace. Because the carnal mind *is* enmity against God; for it is not**

---

37   Matthew 6:10

77

subject to the law of God, nor indeed can be. So then, those who are in the flesh cannot please God.

Romans 8:5-8

Here we find the introduction, awkward as it seems, to spiritual warfare. How do you set your mind on things of the Spirit? First, stop thinking about yourself (the flesh). Desire the things of the Spirit with all your heart; concentrate on that for a while without distraction. Purify and filter your thoughts. Make your mind obey you when it tries to interrupt you with worries or wanders off toward distractions. Use your imagination to meet with God. Jesus explained it this way:

Blessed are the pure in heart, for they shall see God.

Matthew 5:8

You may think "pure in heart" means helpless, infantile or perfect in innocence. But consider that when we recognize our impurities and overcome them, the exercise works up a hunger and thirst for the familiarity of God. Christ purified us, preparing us to enter the presence of the Father. He enables and teaches us to keep our hearts pure by listening to Him. Our willingness to apply a constant purification of our minds and hearts, removing ideas that come against the truth, brings the blessings of a close walk with God Himself. He enjoys spending time with His children, watching them learn new things. When we hang onto His every word, we renew our spirits and shed the old ways. He considers it purity when we sit at the feet of Jesus, our High Priest, learning to use our minds, hearts *and imaginations* for His kingdom.

For though we walk in the flesh, we do not war according to the flesh. For the weapons of our warfare are not carnal but mighty in God for pulling down strongholds, casting down arguments and every high thing that exalts itself against the knowledge of God, bringing every thought into captivity to the obedience of Christ, and being ready to punish all disobedience when your obedience is fulfilled.

2 Corinthians 10:5

In this passage, Paul packed volumes of information about overcoming in the kingdom. One widely misunderstood concept due to translation deserves our attention and focus before we go further: *using your imagination*. If you read this verse in the original King James Version, you'll read **"casting down imaginations and every high thing that exalts itself against the knowledge of God..."** This translation spawned the notion that you should curb your imagination because it might go against the knowledge of God. However, the Greek word **"logismos**[38]**, a reckoning, computation; a reasoning; a judgment, or decision"** gives us a very different meaning from our current concept of imagination. Paul asks us to use our heads. Don't use your emotions or let your imagination take over and run away with you! Add up the facts carefully, reason it out and learn to judge the truth. Then make decisions to throw (cast) out the thoughts and attitudes which create barriers (high things) between you and God's wisdom.

Go ahead and use your imagination if you want to "see" yourself tearing down that wall of pride, brick by brick. Make it permanent, and declare a victory. Work up a sweat in the kingdom! Get in that swift spiritual current and fight against your laziness if you need to. Then go down by the still waters and float effortlessly. Clean up and sit at the feet of the Master to go over your mistakes. Allow Him to teach you how sons and daughters of God behave. If you start to feel proud of your hard-earned accomplishments, cast out that spirit of self-importance. Tear down the walls of resentment, fear, or whatever blocks your relationship with Jesus, thought by thought. Meditate on the precepts of God, learning how He thinks, preparing for the pressures of life in this way.

Now look back at the context of that passage. [39] Paul wrote to the Corinthians urging them to hold onto their faith during their suffering. His letter explained "how" and "why". How do we hold on when we're going through something difficult? We're instructed to **bring every thought** we think **into captivity**. When we do that, then we're ready to move on to greater things in the spiritual battle, such as **punishing disobedient spirits**.

---

38   Strong's G3053, Condensed Brown-Driver-Briggs Hebrew Lexicon, Thayer's Greek Lexicon
39   For context read 2 Corinthians 1:3-7

If we allow distractions to keep us from the mental exercise, we won't be ready for the fight. If we run away from the fight (within ourselves and against our own flesh), or ignore it, we'll starve for the deep knowledge of God.

When we follow that part of the instruction, we find our purpose, "the why" wrapped up in such small victories

Now thanks be to God who always leads us in triumph in Christ, and through us diffuses the fragrance of His knowledge in every place. For we are to God the fragrance of Christ among those who are being saved and among those who are perishing.

2 Corinthians 2:14-15

Learning to diffuse the fragrance of Christ through our actions pleases God! I've thought about that often. Take a deep breath and determine how the smells around you make you *feel*. You get information about activity around you from your senses. At home, we use an aromatherapy diffuser to disburse a pleasant smell of mint, lemon or eucalyptus. Different fragrances seem to change the mood of an individual when they breathe it, allowing the pleasant sensation to overcome the impulse to feel depressed or tired. We cannot prove it works, but anyone who walks through the door inhales deeply. In the same way, your emotions and the spirits they carry put off a fragrance. Whether a spirit of joy or bitterness, humility or arrogance, confidence or worry, it's difficult to hide it. Have you walked into a room and immediately noticed the tension? Some people just put on a cold air of self-centered pride, and others warm the entire room when they walk in with a smile.

Similarly, God diffuses knowledge through us and takes it to a very practical level as we share our stories. We possess the ability to spread hope by sharing God's love for us. People sense a calm and confident spirit. Such knowledge does not convey by words alone, but with excitement in the air because we've overcome an obstacle through the Spirit of Christ! The joy of victory is contagious. Do you spread knowledge in this way? Do you agree that God *always* leads you in triumph through Christ?

If we stop and consider what we share, we often feel inadequate about describing bad circumstances without complaining. During our worst problems it's more important than ever to "diffuse the fragrance" of the knowledge of Christ, and puts the spiritual adversary on notice that we mean business. Begin to describe in a deliberate manner the very real victory that's unfolding because you follow God.

I cannot imagine the suffering and hardship endured by the Corinthians. They stood amid persecutions, even death, believing that God *always* leads in victory through Christ. Not just once in a while or if they prayed hard enough. *Always*. They saw through the physical world into the spirit where God prevails, regardless of appearances in the flesh. These believers used their imagination and took baby steps of obedience to become competent handlers of the truth. They did not wait until they felt ready or their troubles disappeared.

Even now, all logic tells me that I write this Bible study in vain. I know my weaknesses and who will want to listen to me? How will God provide the funds to publish this? But then I hear God saying that He always leads in triumph through Christ, and those who are being saved among the perishing will hear *His voice*, not mine, if I simply follow His instructions. I have to filter out the spirits of doubt from my mind. My willingness to become a fool becomes a fragrant sacrifice to Him. Dear brothers and sisters, whatever you struggle with today, find a way to talk it over with our Father. Ask Christ to help you. You were meant to overcome your spiritual adversaries. God intends for us to triumph!

IDENTIFY YOUR SPIRITUAL ADVERSARIES

One problem with most Christians today is that we simply don't use words to define the adversary at all. We have no idea how to fight or who to fight against. We spend all of our energy with useless complaints against other people instead of defining the moment when we've had it with the demonic spirits that rally against us.

Our thoughts and intentions reveal whether we cooperate with the

Spirit of God or go along with spirits of the flesh. If the power of the Holy Spirit is at work in us, then our life proves it.

But you are not in the flesh but in the Spirit, if indeed the Spirit of God dwells in you. Now if anyone does not have the Spirit of Christ, he is not His. And if Christ *is* in you, the body *is* dead because of sin, but the Spirit *is* life because of righteousness.

Romans 8:9-10

In this letter to the Romans, Paul wrote to both Gentiles and Jews. He put effort into explaining the purpose of the Torah to the Gentiles. Then he offered special cautions to those who knew the laws of God.[40] He knew they could find in Christ a much deeper faith because they already understood the concept of obedience to God's word. He wanted them to distinguish between spiritual maturity and legalistic religious conformity, seeking a deeper relationship with God as the goal. He cautioned them not to try these spiritual things for self-serving reasons (pride of flesh) or personal gain. Instead, he taught them to use the power and authority of the kingdom to put the deeds of the body to death.

But if the Spirit of Him who raised Jesus from the dead dwells in you, He who raised Christ from the dead will also give life to your mortal bodies through His Spirit who dwells in you. Therefore, brethren, we are debtors—not to the flesh, to live according to the flesh. For if you live according to the flesh you will die; but if by the Spirit you put to death the deeds of the body, you will live.

Romans 8:11-13

You see, Paul understood the struggle. He lived it wholeheartedly. He submitted his own life in obedience and excellence, forcing himself to comply with God's laws to attain righteousness. Yet when Christ showed him what he was missing, he opted for the great power and authority that

---

40   Find the context of Paul's statements in Romans 7:1

comes only through the Holy Spirit.

When we make choices, we *feel* as if we're in control of own our life. We see the consequences and mark our own progress and failure. However, when we try to control ourselves rather than giving in to the Holy Spirit's control, Paul tells us that we oppose God! **"Now if anyone does not have the Spirit of Christ, he is not His."** Stop and think about that. **"For if you live according to the flesh you will die."** Paul hammered this point to the more knowledgeable audiences often, because it's easy to miss the best part. **"...if by the Spirit you put to death the deeds of the body, you will live."** We can receive the power and authority that controls the flesh while we're here. We know he spoke about eternal life, but don't miss the entire point of his message: overcoming the spirits while we live in the flesh.

I get so excited when I read these passages. It means that every little victory counts. I've conquered spirits in ways that don't appear victorious to anyone but me; but I know what spirits I've overcome. I know how I held my tongue when every fiber of my being told me to speak the obvious. I felt the stab of truth pierce my heart when my tongue took control. I learned to practice filtering out and discarding unloving thoughts when I detected them. I force my mouth to build up instead of staying silent. I really saw the malicious devils of pain trying to thwart my victory when I injured my spine. Without the Spirit's power and authority, I might be limping into pain management clinics for pharmaceutical remedies. Instead, God allowed me to demonstrate His power over my flesh, participate in His victory, share the story and declare His glory. Every day I wake up to new challenges and an exhilarating hike in the kingdom. When I fall, I get up and get back on the trail, asking Christ to teach me, renewing my mind as I go further.

We try to see physical evidence of spiritual activity in other believers. We look for examples of godly people experiencing this victorious lifestyle, and find them disguised in humility and harsh circumstances, living on the front lines of spiritual battles.

If we attempt to put to death the deeds of the body on our own strength and succeed at it, will we live? **No.** We'll wake up every day and start over with the same struggle. We can make it look good and try to appear religious, but it's still vain deceit. It wears us out and leads to death. Only the Spirit of Christ gives us victory over death and authority in the spirit world. We experience spiritual victory when we become completely dependent upon God.

> **He delivered me from my strong enemy, from those who hated me; for they were too strong for me. They confronted me in the day of my calamity, but the Lord was my support.**
> **2 Samuel 22:18-19**

The earth and the flesh represent the *Todays* of our eternity.[41] Go past confusion about whether it's more important to have faith or good works; recognize your salvation as the point of entry, the gate of God's kingdom. Suppose you believe in Christ and accept His saving grace. You give Him control and turn away from your errors. You begin to mature a little at a time, understanding more about how your Father thinks by reading His laws. If you *accidentally* put your own (carnal) desires over God's Laws, does His Spirit lose control? No, He simply gives you freedom of choice.

He's like a loving father allowing you to practice steering while you learn to drive under his watch. He wants you to gain skills in spiritual power, but because it's unseen, you miss the mark sometimes. That's sin, but not outright rebellion. You keep improving and perfecting as you *choose* to give the Spirit control of your mind. His spiritual eyesight is much better than your earthly vision, and shows you the way to inner peace and the rewards of the eternal kingdom of heaven.

Conversely, if we allow our thoughts to be controlled by the flesh (world around us), our actions lead to death. Saying we believe in Him brings about no change unless we go into the gates of the kingdom and follow Him. We must imitate Him closely and learn to outsmart devils. He'll show us how to love and forgive our enemies, heaping coals on the heads of their deceiving spirits.

A prideful spirit might cause a person to say that following the Way seems like a mindless exercise for those who cannot think for themselves.

---

41   Hebrews 3-4

However, if one refuses to let the Spirit of God lead them, they allow the flesh to lead them by default. The choice begins in the mind, either way. If someone takes in knowledge without understanding, they sometimes miss the truth that comes with wisdom.

Which one takes more effort? I cannot imagine a more preposterous or difficult position to defend than Judeo-Christianity. It defies rational explanation, and yet every word of it rings true. God really loves us and wants a relationship with every person. He adopts as His children all those who choose to love Him back. He makes no distinction between the simple minded and highly intelligent.

Clean or unclean, Christ purifies all individuals who come to Him. Saints or prostitutes,[42] rich or poor, Jew or Gentile, God's invitation to join Him defies logic. And if that's not enough to convince you that it is impossible without Him, listen to this: He expects us all to love each other and unite as one family!

Make no mistake, if you follow the Way, you must become skilled at thinking differently, retraining your mind to hear God instead of the repetitive echo of the world. Followers of the Way become the offspring of God. Such wholehearted trust leads to this dynamic way of life. Don't get stuck in the same old thought patterns that cause you to shrink back in fear of the devil's discomfort.

For as many as are led by the Spirit of God, these are sons of God. For you did not receive the spirit of bondage again to fear, but you received the Spirit of adoption by whom we cry out, "Abba, Father."

Romans 8:14-15.

God gives us a sense of peace during our earthly struggles between the power of the flesh and the power of the Spirit because He *is* peace. We rest only when we let Him direct our minds. The Way (Jesus Himself) lives in us! The Way is not a path; it's a person we choose to live with, listen to and follow.

Jesus simply says, **"Follow Me."**

---

42   Joshua 2

THE ART OF OVERCOMING

There is therefore now no condemnation to those who are in Christ Jesus, who do not walk according to the flesh, but according to the Spirit.

Romans 8:1

Dare to give serious consideration to Paul's statement about walking according to the Spirit. Neither time nor space exists in the spirit world, yet while we live in a fleshy body, Christ's Spirit gives us a new way to walk. We do not start out walking perfectly, and need a lifetime of practice. However, when we fall down or stray off the course, we lose our way, not our identity. This "no condemnation" clause allows for our refinement when we accidentally walk according to the flesh. That's where grace comes in again and again, as our Father gives us a chance to mature and learn. God gives us grace unto salvation. When it comes to our judgment, however, God knows if we really did our best, or if we didn't show up for practice.

You see, God sent His Spirit so we could succeed as His offspring. He does not want to condemn us! The art of balancing our tendency to fall back on that grace, and learning to master the flesh at the same time, pushing forward in faith, allows us to participate in this creative process.

Every believer knows that their job requires travel. We need to follow Christ. However, we often follow each other instead, failing to walk in the commands of God. God enacted the laws to identify sin, so we would clearly know the difference between good and evil. We need to know. No matter how mature our faith, God continues to reveal new ways to glorify Him as we discover and root out our own errors.

Christ actually fulfills God's law in this way each time a person invites His Spirit to enter into them to teach! This activity erases time, space, and our chances of failure; it puts all the emphasis on growing up as children of God. His Spirit shows us how to walk as we go. We take the first step, then the second... Occasionally we stumble.

I want to live in the spirit now, but I must constantly guard against corruption of the flesh. While the world floods me with distractions, my Bible tells me to forget about the appearance of my transitory earthly life and look beyond. The Old Testament tells me to keep order, cleanliness and godliness in my life while I honor God. The New Testament goes further to teach me to live *in my spirit*.

The corruption of the flesh seems natural and real when I experience pain or emotion. It tries to get all of my attention with food and pleasure. My body would take over my entire life if I did not put up a fight against it and make it obey my spirit.

Scripture says God spoke everything into being. He thought of us long before He put His breath in us. Throughout eternity He's waited for our time to choose Him, walk with Him, and wake up with Him in our thoughts.

Notice that you cannot walk His way and your own way at the same time. He'll gradually reveal the secrets of the kingdom when you attempt to imitate Him (follow). By making a conscious effort to walk first in the spirit, you automatically cause something to change in the natural as a consequence. The deceiver confuses people about spiritual work, but God laid out clear and concise spiritual laws. Certain choices lead to death, others lead to eternal life.

For this commandment which I command you today is not too mysterious for you, nor is it far off. It is not in heaven, that you should say, "Who will ascend into heaven for us and bring it to us, that we may hear it and do it?" ... but the word is very near you, in your mouth and in your heart, that you may do it. See, I have set before you today life and good, death and evil, in that I command you today to love the LORD your God, to walk in His ways, and to keep His commandments, His statutes, and His judgments, that you may live...

Deuteronomy 30:11-16a

Living strictly in the slow moving molecules of the flesh, the lines seem blurred. We feel a need to do many things at the same time, or nothing at all, because none of these actions satisfy us for long. We've developed a society of commerce and productivity fueled by this desire to multitask in the physical realm. Without the invisible light-speed force of God's imagination behind the technology, none of it would exist. Yet our generation managed to build a system of image worship like none other in history. Imagine God's disappointment, when He created us to do so much more with our knowledge in the spirit. Jesus, the Word, is near us, in our mouths, in our hearts, on the tips of our tongues!

Walking in the flesh, we go with the flow of the world and refuse to discern the spirits that God wants us to oppose. Instead, we ignore them. The world says they don't exist; God expects us to recognize them when they interfere.

Make a distinction between "walking in" the flesh and "overcoming" the flesh. Discern the spirits that corrupt the heart and mind. Refuse to give in to them. *Overcome* the carnal emotions that vie for your attention. Spiritual beings must put effort into seeing things differently. That's overcoming.

I need to pause here and confess that it's not as easy as it sounds, for as soon as we conquer one wayward thought and feel like celebrating, another one comes to mind and tries to escape through our mouth! Ours is not a passive faith. It takes practice to experience a peace-filled spirit, although it's a free gift for the taking. If you accept Christ as your savior but then refuse the power of His Spirit to conquer your flesh, you cannot please God in the way that He planned. Your Father will discipline and correct you as His child, until you learn to listen to Him. Jesus wants you to gain victory over the adversary.

> **You have turned for me my mourning into dancing; You have put off my sackcloth and clothed me with gladness, to the end that my glory may sing praise to You and not be silent.**
>
> **Psalm 30:11-12**

The Way involves honest decisions to follow God's voice (walking in the Spirit) and overcoming (real spiritual warfare). Believing in Him and following Him are not the same. Believers become children of God by following Him. Any time we allow our fleshy desires to take over our mind, we cannot possibly walk with God because He is Spirit. He sends help when we struggle and call out to Him. He fights for us when we put Him first.

> **The LORD your God, who goes before you, He will fight for you, according to all He did for you in Egypt before your eyes, and in the wilderness where you saw how the LORD your God carried you, as a man carries his son, in all the way that you went until you came to this place.**
>
> **Deuteronomy 1:30-31**

We need to understand this process to follow the Way, because when God goes out in front of us, the struggle ends decisively. When you realize how this works, you want to practice it. The fine art of overcoming opens you up to the power of the Holy Spirit. By listening and following God's directions, your authority grows in the spirit world. You *walk* in it and Christ reveals what you can bear each day. When you feel tired, Daddy picks you up and carries you.

WALKING WITH THE FATHER

None of us can *lead* the way, no matter how wise we become, for as soon as we start thinking about leading other people, we try to run out in front of God again. By making plans and concentrating on details, we put the material world first. Instead, we only need to point ahead and say, "I'm following God. Look what He is doing!"

Our Father still loves us regardless of our progress in our walk, but He's already set His spiritual laws in motion. They affect the physical outcome. In the spirit, Jesus and His Father are working all the time.[43] However, in the material world, He already created all He needs. The pattern of working and resting *simultaneously* reveals our God-given personality.

Isn't it just like God to give us free will? His artistic flair combines with our choices to determine the shape and pattern of our lives, renewing every cell as we go through the process! If we cooperate with Him completely, He changes and re-shapes us until we gain power to overcome the flesh, experience peace and practice the mysteries of the kingdom of God.

Victory rests with the LORD.

Proverbs 21:31

Victory does not rest upon our level of mastery or the circumstances around us. Triumphs come only after we submit ourselves to His discipline. Our ultimate success depends upon whom we serve: (a) the flesh and desires of the world, OR (b) the Spirit of the Living God.

God's law teaches and corrects our thinking so that we live in right relationship with Him and each other. It points out the weakness of the flesh, lest we forget the temporary nature of our bodies. Paul said it this way:

I find then a law, that evil is present with me, the one who wills to do good. For I delight in the law of God according to the inward man. But I see another law in my members, warring

---

43   John 5:17

against the law of my mind, and bringing me into captivity to the law of sin which is in my members. O wretched man that I am! Who will deliver me from this body of death? I thank God- through Jesus Christ our Lord! So then, with the mind I myself serve the law of God, but with the flesh the law of sin.

Romans 7:21-25

By the external standard of the law, we all stand guilty and condemned to death. The law of God, written on the tablets of our souls, becomes our code of conduct in His family. We know it in our hearts and read the Bible for directions. When we put our flesh first, we experience the results of the law of sin. This does not mean that "we lost our salvation" as a believer. (Remember, salvation is our point of entry into the kingdom of power and authority, not something to gain or lose by our actions.) But we cannot rest in this condition, because we lost our way or never entered the gate to begin with. He wired us to continue to seek Him until we get into the Rest, the holy Sabbath that satisfies our soul with purpose. We gain confidence in the new covenant when we fully embrace the Way.

When God expects us to overcome, He'll show us how to do it. Not expecting us to know our way around the kingdom right away, He wants us to submit to His leadership. You see, we find peace only when we take up the good fight and learn to use our spiritual weapons. We do not fight against *people* who break the law (unless we belong to a branch of law enforcement). In the spirit, however, we must overcome any spirits that come against us. We declare war on our own flesh and **cut off any part of our life that leads us to sin.** That repellent doctrine causes us to procrastinate until our problems require action.

The Holy Spirit teaches us how to use power and authority to overcome the spirits that lead to death and darkness. He shows us how to set up sensitive surveillance devices in our mind to detect them and overthrow them quickly. Repentance really means realizing you're going nowhere with your own methods and changing your direction to follow Christ. Make up your mind about the Way of your life.

Never, ever give up the struggle to overcome the flesh, to put it in second place in your life. Your body serves as a tabernacle of worship, a connection with God through your mind. When you start wondering why your circumstances have not changed much, don't be disappointed. God put you there for a reason. Look in the spirit to see Him working all around you. He wants to involve you in spiritual work, and will show you the real fight against your enemies in His kingdom. Jesus told the disciples:

> **If the world hates you, you know that it hated Me before *it hated* you. If you were of the world, the world would love its own. Yet because you are not of the world, but I chose you out of the world, therefore the world hates you.**
>
> **John 15:18-19**

As we begin to make our flesh obey us, we realize that we're not from here. We follow Jesus and His Spirit teaches us to overcome, the ultimate goal of all faithful people. His Spirit moves into us to provide strength and power *only if we cooperate* with Him. (Follow.)

After salvation, God continues to give us freedom to choose our own "level" of obedience. We decide whether we control our tongue or say whatever comes to mind. We choose to listen for His directions or not. We decide if we have time to do what we hear Him tell us to do. If we don't feel like making the effort, then suddenly we're walking in the flesh again! We bear the consequences of these choices.

Our mind cannot be *against* God and *for* Him at the same time. The Holy Spirit does not control us when we live life with no intention of following God's commands. No, we've taken back the control of our spirit and we're living in the flesh again. God commands His servants in the kingdom to watch over us and report back to Him. After all, He loves us and wants us to keep practicing until we trust God's love.

Christ Himself promised to mediate for us, and when His Spirit falls upon us, He teaches us the mysteries of eternal life. He knows these lessons must first deal with our fears, our laziness and our desire for comfort; thus He tests us on these minor levels until we learn to overcome our earthly way of handling problems.

MARKED WITH A SEAL

His Spirit gives us the only way into the kingdom. It helped me to understand this better by exploring my pre-conceived ideas about the Holy Spirit. God's Spirit of unsearchable power and mystery makes us aware of how little we understand, and how much we need Him to navigate in the kingdom. Walking in the Spirit of Christ, we glimpse our part in the earthly drama where we *become* children of God. His Spirit directs our exploration of the kingdom.[44]

The Greeks in Ephesus received a letter from Paul explaining some of these deep mysteries of scripture. The short book of Ephesians gives us clues about the nature of Holy Spirit. In this letter, Paul put a lot of effort into giving us a vision of a united spiritual household, the body of Christ.

Our secular ideas about individuality hinder us from understanding the mystery of the Holy Spirit. In other words, how do you see past your "self" in your relationship with the Holy Ghost? How does He connect us to the body of Christ? Neither time nor space constrains the Spirit of God, yet we're limited to both in our language and perception. To understand the activity of this inexplicable spiritual union, we should try to make a distinction between physical and spiritual. In simplistic terms, *when* we receive the Holy Spirit, Christ lives in us from that day forward. (See how we need to use time to measure our realities?) Yet we find few people who truly walk in His power and authority[45]- and possess the knowledge and experience to teach by example. I know this grieves the Holy Spirit. Theology experts, priests, preachers and teachers have speculated as to why this happened, but no one knows for sure. The adversary covered up the knowledge and now we shall recover whatever Christ reveals to us by His Spirit. It's a mystery. Read Paul's words in Ephesians and go past the veil to sit at the feet of the Master while He teaches something important.

Understand how the Spirit groans with our refusal to walk in unity with Him. Think about what we've learned about "walking" in the Spirit as you read this:

---

44   Ephesians 4:11-16
45   John 14:12

Let no corrupt word proceed out of your mouth, but what is good for necessary edification, that it may impart grace to the hearers, and do not grieve the Holy Spirit of God, by whom you were sealed for the day of redemption.

Ephesians 4:29-30

The Spirit moves about like the wind and goes where it pleases, without regard to time and space. Your salvation does not come and go. You're marked with a seal in the spiritual kingdom if you trust in Christ Jesus, and this signifies for all eternity that you're part of the family of Abraham. The angels and demons of heaven interact with you as He commands them, urging, bringing messages, testing you...

If you believe that the Spirit was sealed in you after you accepted Christ, ask God to reveal what this means to you. You cannot confine the Holy Spirit, sealed up within your soul like He's in a zip-lock bag! Search the scriptures and read for context. He will disclose more to you about your relationship with Him if you really seek the truth.

During Biblical times, the king placed a seal of wax on an important document, putting the imprint from his ring on the wax to indicate that it was authentic. The importance of the seal was twofold: It indicated who wrote the letter or owned the package, and it meant that the contents had valuable information about the kingdom. If the king's son wore a similar ring, it signified his ability to manage the affairs of his father. The seal carried authority in the kingdom. No one denied or ignored the seal of the king under penalty of the law.

In the spiritual kingdom, this seal gives you right of entry. As you mature in faith, becoming a son or daughter of God, this seal makes it possible for you to work with authority over the entire kingdom. Show up for your lessons to become more like Him and gain the right to use His Name. Christ's Spirit gives you direct access to your Father as you begin to overcome![46]

We do not possess, keep or lose the Holy Spirit. As for our physical bodies and our souls, we can make ourselves available. We serve as

---

46   John 16:12-23

containers for our Father's pleasure, because it pleases Him to dwell in us. The entire kingdom of heaven (loaded with angels and demons, principalities and powers) resides within us too.

When we follow the path that Christ laid out for us, the blessings already await us. If we choose to believe *in Him* but do not believe all of His promises, we choose weakness of the flesh instead of power in the Holy Spirit.

> **Who is wise and understanding among you? Let him show by good conduct that his works are done in the meekness of wisdom. But if you have bitter envy and self-seeking in your hearts, do not boast and lie against the truth. This wisdom does not descend from above, but is earthly, sensual, demonic. For where envy and self-seeking exist, confusion and every evil thing are there.**
>
> **James 3:13-16**

I wonder how our senses might lead to corruption. We need to consider this verse again, realizing that James wrote to believers in the congregation. Christians feel exempt from the *evil* and *demonic* because of the power of the Holy Spirit. The Spirit enables us to overcome them. The short list of characteristics - envy, self-seeking, confusion, and every evil thing- surely these work their way into the church on the backs of people carrying prideful "wisdom". Those early believers worked hard for the gospel, endured persecutions and narrowly escaped Jerusalem with their families.[47] Most of them knew the scriptures from childhood. They seemed wise; but their hearts, like ours, were prone to egocentric behavior when they experienced victory. Envy and selfishness led to confusion and every evil thing.

Any time we work for the church with our focus on the earthly outcome, we're not using our senses for spiritual purposes. Any time we fall into a religious routine that leads to our own self-fulfillment, we give place to the demonic. Search the scriptures with an eye for the original language,

---

47   Acts 8:1, 11:19

setting and context if you're rushing to correct me. Most believers, not understanding the nature of demons, think that such spirits have no place in them if they are truly saved, but scripture indicates that they roam the earth seeking people to inhabit,[48] hitching a ride on little white lies and envious thoughts.

Created by God, and operating under His authority, they affect your life. Don't give them an inch. Resist demons, learn to overcome them and they'll spur you on to new growth. Who is wise among you? See how easily they take over when you give them a place. Understand that you choose what to do next when you recognize them. Cast them out or prepare for discipline. Fill up the space they left behind with God's living word and set up a proper defense system for your earthly outpost.

Maturing, we develop a pattern of consistent obedience by listening to our Father's voice. His children increase in knowledge of His kingdom with a clear purpose for God, walking in peace during turmoil. He measures our intentions, words and works as we develop.

We measure our babies to see if they grow, don't we? We give tests in school to see if students pay attention, and God evaluates our continuing progress, too. Listen to the warning Christ gives to the church:

> **...I know your works, that you have a name that you are alive, but you are dead. Be watchful, and strengthen the things which remain, that are ready to die, for I have not found your works perfect before God. Remember therefore how you have received and heard; hold fast and repent. Therefore if you will not watch, I will come upon you as a thief, and you will not know what hour I will come upon you.**
>
> **Revelation 3:1b-3**

Some people have lost the desire to grow. They go around with such unrepentant spirits that they simply stop growing. Jesus warns us. He hates that we call ourselves Christians with no intention of following God's laws. We try to represent Him with unremorseful spirits and use

---

48   Luke 11:24

His name to pray in vain. Our works are imperfect because of it. We have His Name, but we're not using it for kingdom business with the power and precision of His Spirit. He's telling us there's more to it than feeling good in the worship service. Go beyond the veil and walk with Christ. Take the training and get your uniform.

> **You have a few names even in Sardis who have not defiled their garments; and they shall walk with Me in white, for they are worthy. He who overcomes shall be clothed in white garments, and I will not blot out his name from the Book of Life; but I will confess his name before My Father and before His angels.**
>
> **Revelation 3:4-5**

If you want to know what God expects us to do in the family business, "overcoming" describes a big part of our job. We start out small and polish our skills to gain proficiency. At our salvation, Jesus gave us beautiful white garments, but we've walked in the flesh again and gotten them dirty. Jesus says to wash up and come into the kingdom to walk with Him. Don't go back into that filth this time. If you get dirty again, repent. Clean up, don't cover up. Jesus prepares you to meet with the Father.

THE YOKE

Jesus explained complex truths with genius simplicity. If you feel burdened, He offers the easy yoke as a practical tool to use in any situation.

The word yoke brings to mind a pair of huge oxen with a heavy wooden yoke strapped to their backs, pulling a burden too large for a man. The thought of carrying any kind of yoke, even a light and easy one, repels us. But let's take another look at our burdens and learn to handle them in a new way.

If we pray, "Lord, carry this for me," we wait to see what happens. This prayer of the new believer brings forth heavenly intervention in times of need. As we begin to mature spiritually, however, God expects us to take the sacred responsibility of our words and actions.[49] Sometimes, God chooses not to carry our burdens so that we will increase in character and righteousness. In the same way, when you exercise with weights, you gradually add to the amount of resistance to improve your muscle tone. These burdens represent tests, and Jesus our teacher, gave us extraordinary insight into handling them.

The events surrounding His statements about the yoke are important. John the Baptist had sent him a message from prison. You can hear Jesus' frustration as He talked about the way people respond to the truth.

---

49   Matthew 25:14-30

For John came neither eating nor drinking, and they say, 'He has a demon.' The Son of Man came eating and drinking, and they say, 'Look, a glutton and a winebibber, a friend of tax collectors and sinners!' But wisdom is justified by her children.

Matthew 11:18-19

Then Jesus began to reprimand some of the cities where He had performed miracles and people did not repent or change. Listen to the sorrow in His voice as He considers the multitudes that rejected His message.

But I say to you that it shall be more tolerable for the land of Sodom in the day of judgment than for you.

Matthew 11:24

You can almost hear Him take a deep breath and pause to talk to God:

I thank You, Father, Lord of heaven and earth, that You have hidden these things from *the* wise and prudent and have revealed them to babes. Even so, Father, for so it seemed good in Your sight.

Matthew 11:25-26

Then He directed these words to the crowd:

All things have been delivered to Me by My Father, and no one knows the Son except the Father. Nor does anyone know the Father except the Son, and *the one* to whom the Son wills to reveal *Him.* Come to Me, all *you* who labor and are heavy laden, and I will give you rest. Take My yoke upon you and learn from Me, for I am gentle and lowly in heart, and you will find rest for your souls. For My yoke *is* easy and My burden is light.

Matthew 11:27-30

Dissatisfied with the faithlessness of people who were diligently expecting their Messiah to appear, Jesus thought of children. Consider the differences between adults and children to understand His analogy. As babies, we begin in this world totally fresh and new, absorbing our surroundings as pure innocent sponges. We are carefree and trusting. During the first part of our childhood, we laugh easily and cry often. We feel deeply. We internalize everything we see, smell, touch, taste and hear to make it part of us. We learn by exercising our senses.[50]

Brought into the world helpless, babies begin life totally dependent upon the love and care of their parents. When they finally earn the right to accept responsibility, they don't think of it as a burden, but rather an honor, a challenge that gives them a sense of mission and purpose. Adults experience anxiety about change, associating it with discomfort. In contrast, toddlers generally savor life's experiences. They keep repeating and practicing, fall after fall. They seem to enjoy the game of learning with a sense of accomplishment. Perhaps they feel no pressure because they trust their parents to watch out for them as they learn.

Small children consider any burden a gift of great value. They embrace the opportunity to carry something important or heavy with innocent enthusiasm. Their eyes light up with delight when someone presents them with responsibility. They have a way of taking it without feeling any ownership. This sort of detachment removes all of the mental pressure and frees them to live with abandon. If we "become as little children," we shift our burdens. Our Father gives us access to His mysterious yoke, with power to turn the greatest burden into a privilege and honor reserved only to those who trust Him.

But what do we do with all of our troubles? How do we sort them out? We certainly can't see them as a privilege from where we stand! Problems, past experiences, and the way we see ourselves handling our challenges, combine to produce tension in adults. Tension, as you may know, should be adjusted properly, or it will snap. We accumulate things, collect experiences and find the task of keeping them prioritized overwhelming. We constantly strive to live in the present and overcome our failures and shortcomings from the past. We seem happier if we balance it well.

When our needs consume our thoughts, we tend to allow our focus to

---

50   Hebrews 5:14

get out of perspective. Our search for meaning becomes meaningless. It, too, becomes a huge burden. The easy yoke puts purpose in every problem and gives us momentum to keep going. Jesus' yoke removes the sense of heaviness about mistakes and gives us the means to live within His laws. Our happiness and health depend upon our capacity to see past our limitations and our surroundings, into the bigger picture. Humble and vulnerable, we can yoke ourselves with our Creator, instead of trying to carry our own accomplishments. He purchased us from our slavery to the world. We connect ourselves to Him and follow His timeless precepts instead.

God watches us rushing, here and there, and continues to remind us of His master plan for eternity. Whatever we do, it probably doesn't impress God. No, but He's encouraging us with every new step toward Him. When we read His words in the Bible, we learn that He loves us deeply. As His offspring, He gives us credit for listening to Him and imitating Christ. When His Spirit moves us into action, it lifts us beyond our own human strength or wisdom. It supersedes our impulse to drown our sorrows or get caught up in merriment and distractions. Jesus reminds us of the unthinkable end of the world as we know it.

But take heed to yourselves, lest your hearts be weighed down with carousing, drunkenness, and cares of this life, and that Day come on you unexpectedly.

Luke 21:34

He urges us to live life with a new outlook, seeing each new day as a privilege instead of a burden. He cautions us to let go of the baggage that weighs down our hearts and makes us feel unlucky or slighted. He tells us to rise to the occasion by relinquishing any control we thought we desired over the physical world, that final burden of human beings. Begin to see the big picture, where angels fight for our souls and God numbered each of our human hairs. Jesus reminds us to serve each other with joy... to become as little children.

FORGIVING THE UNFORGIVABLE

Jesus gave *very specific* instructions to handle difficult relationships of all kinds. Encouraging us to communicate with those who have offended us, He insists that we look deeply at our personal relationships.

> **Take heed to yourselves. If your brother sins against you, rebuke him; and if he repents, forgive him. And if he sins against you seven times in a day, and seven times in a day returns to you, saying, 'I repent,' you shall forgive him.**
>
> **Luke 17:3-4**

From the extreme deception to the subtle omission, God expects us to look each other squarely in the eyes and say, "You hurt me," "I'm sorry," and "I forgive you." Granted, that's a tough one if it just keeps happening again and again. You might think that communication skills need to improve *a lot* for this method to do any good in your situation. Nevertheless, I must remind myself, and you, that we're not talking about a method, but rather a divine intervention, when we obey these Biblical instructions. His love pours out the grace to forgive others and we're required to use this for the kingdom.[51] Until we practice this wholeheartedly, we block our own blessings, too.

Blessed is he whose transgression is forgiven, whose sin is covered. Blessed is the man to whom the LORD does not impute iniquity, and in whose spirit there is no deceit.

Psalm 32:1-2

When we get to the point that we can only see a person in terms of how they have hurt us, we really need a change. We can't act in good faith if we doubt the outcome. Our faith develops into hope for the promises of God, but these promises do not manifest without effort.

If we think they'll do it again, how can we follow Jesus' teaching? Adjust your heart to beat in rhythm with the Spirit of God so that you always forgive. Repentance and forgiveness create a synergy of healing power. Jesus taught us to use them in our relationships.

The path to forgiveness starts within us. It's all about our relationship with God, Himself. If you try to forgive just by *saying* that you forgive, you'll carry that hurt around forever. Maybe you *tried* to forgive someone by changing your attitude toward them, but now, if you're serious, you'll want to go further to get the blessings of obedience from your Father. Whether you've buried deep wounds from childhood or participated in a minor quarrel, you need Christ to make the way smooth, seamless and eternal.

Jesus calls us into our temple within to work on the basics of forgiveness. Root out deceiving spirits that lead you into sin, and get rid of blame altogether. Once you identify these devils, the next step requires true repentance, a commitment to change your thinking. Go past your negative emotions to overcome the spirits behind them. Admit that they're affecting you and quit feeding them! Starve them out. You may find hidden shame and abuses too painful to bear, or the same fearful thoughts that keep popping into your mind. Jesus cleaned them out when you first believed, but you may have opened a way for them due to a lack of knowledge of God's word.

---

51   Psalm 51:13

Warning: Sinful spirits attached to feelings of regret, bitterness and blame will fight to their death to keep you down, but they hold no power over the Holy Spirit. You can overcome them when you are ready to face them. Don't give up. Let Him show you how to send them away forever. Pursue them instead of trying to avoid them in your kingdom. Christ shows us how to sever their connection by removing spiritual ties to all regrets and mistakes.

Now, recognize this kingdom-activity as part of repentance and look at the mental process that accompanies it. Confessing to God, we tell Him of our sorrow for our part, however large or small, in the offense, and beg for His mercy. We recognize how our bad attitude affected other people. We ask Christ to help us stay clean from here forward. Where we once blamed, we apply love instead. Forgiven by God, atoned by the blood of Jesus Christ, we're completely free from the disappointment that we kept locked inside us. He teaches us to fill up with His love until it crowds out all past mistakes.

Our world says not to follow Him. Our mind tells us it's crazy to forgive repeatedly. Our society says it's dangerous, and that may be true. Know this: when you stand in opposition to the evil in the world, the Creator Himself and His legions of angels back you up.

For He shall give His angels charge over you, to keep you in all your ways. In *their* hands they shall bear you up, lest you dash your foot against a stone.

Psalm 91:11-12

Follow Jesus' path of forgiveness with confidence. It takes persistence to live that kind of faith in everyday communication with people. Especially when our burdens loom larger than life and we feel like giving up on someone and discarding them. Jesus doesn't want us to give up on each other! He can change us, heal our wounds and give us a new way of life. Then He uses us to distribute the fragrance of forgiveness. We must begin with those we already know. In this way, God shows up in our relationships.

No man has ever seen God; if we love one another, God abides in us and His love is perfected in us.

1 John 4:12

As we communicate compassion and forgiveness over and over to those we love, Jesus recommends patience. They may continue to react in the old ways for some time, but never give up. Always expect a miracle. Plant seeds of faith everywhere. Keep watering them, expecting a great and mighty outcome. Offer grace to everyone you know. Even if you never see the change in that person's life, recognize that the seed of God's love softens in them each time *you* obey. Difficult people in our lives may stretch our patience to the limit, but if we approach them with integrity and find ways to honestly love them, we develop spiritual muscles as we work through our problems together.

What do you do about your own past mistakes? Face them and acknowledge them. Then talk to God openly about them, ask His forgiveness and reject any regretful pent up emotions. Let the people you hurt go free; ask them, if possible, to forgive you. Forgive yourself. If you look back at a dark time in your life with regret, remember that Jesus went to extremes to bring you back to Him. Remember **hatta't?**[52] Accept His forgiveness and look at His example:

... when He was reviled, did not revile in return; when He suffered, He did not threaten, but committed *Himself* to Him who judges righteously; who Himself bore our sins in His own body on the tree, that we, having died to sins, might live for righteousness—by whose stripes you were healed. For you were like sheep going astray, but have now returned to the Shepherd and Overseer of your souls.

1 Peter 2:23-25

Jesus healed us with His suffering and made it possible to start fresh with His Spirit as the Overseer of our soul. He gave us a new lease on our

---

52   This Hebrew word for sin implies both "sin" and "sin offering", and indicates that God planned a way out from our bad choices.

earthly life, and more importantly, a sealed ownership in an eternal place in heaven.

> **But this *is* the covenant that I will make with the house of Israel after those days, says the LORD: I will put My law in their minds, and write it on their hearts; and I will be their God, and they shall be My people. No more shall every man teach his neighbor, and every man his brother, saying, 'Know the LORD,' for they all shall know Me, from the least of them to the greatest of them, says the LORD. For I will forgive their iniquity, and their sin I will remember no more.**
>
> **Jeremiah 31:33-34**

God knows what the future looks like. At some point, He sees all people cooperating in a spirit of love, fully knowing His law. The truth that settles all disputes about right and wrong shall permeate our collective consciousness, and settle all theological debate. We'll all tremble before Him as we see His magnificent plan unfold into real peace on earth. For now, God forgives the shortcomings of His sincere believers when they repent. He wants them to remember their identity as "doers" of the word.[53]

When you learn the lessons of the mind and heart from Him, the first thing you notice may take you by surprise. Your religious zeal dissolves into the loving forgiveness of our Father. Instead of strict enforcement of doctrines and traditions, you find that He urges you to follow Him to a greater destiny of humble service.

FORGIVE YOUR WAY TO ANSWERED PRAYERS.

Jesus spoke candidly to the disciples about the importance of forgiveness, and how it affects our prayer power. One day they walked by a fig tree with no fruit. He was hungry and spoke a curse to the tree, "Let no one eat fruit from you ever again." The next day they came by the tree, completely withered, and they asked Him how He did it. He explained that such power starts with inward preparation: faith, whole-hearted belief and forgiveness.

---

53   James 1:23-24

And whenever you stand praying, if you have anything against anyone, forgive him, that your Father in heaven may also forgive you your trespasses. But if you do not forgive, neither will your Father in heaven forgive your trespasses.

Mark 11:25

If you really want your prayers to be heard, faith in God is not enough. Your willingness to sweep your house clean by forgiving comes first! Let's explore that truth further. Follow Jesus, the boy, as He grew, experiencing what it felt like to obey His own laws. As a youth, He walked to the synagogue each morning with His father before daybreak to study Torah with the other men. Then they went out into the fields to chop down trees, saw lumber, haul, sand, and build. He listened to the stories of the wise men as they talked. Born into humble circumstances, His family worked hard all week and then stopped everything on Saturdays to worship God and rest. Celebrating the Holy Days and following the customs of the Israelites, He saw the difference between the commands of God and the traditions passed down to help people obey God's laws. While some of His teachers were strict legalists, Jesus the Messiah opened the way with a message of forgiveness where all people can share the warmth of God's love.

Jesus offers a deeper faith and teaches us to go much further than the minimum requirements of the Laws. The commanded Holy Days of Rosh Hashanah and Yom Kippur picture what God had in mind about forgiveness. Members of the community take an entire month to go to one another, make amends for misunderstandings and seek forgiveness. Whether you've offended someone or caught them lying, you talk it out and forgive each other, agreeing to make amends and correct the wrong. On the great day of Yom Kippur the community comes before God with clean hearts concerning their brothers and sisters. Then they ask for forgiveness for any sins, corporate and individual, that they may have committed against God. Isn't this a picture of what God expects our churches to look like today?

God, the Father, commands that we forgive. Jesus, the Man, forgave.

Jesus, the Teacher, explained why we need to forgive. Jesus, the Messiah, pointed to complete forgiveness as the key to spiritual power. *Our sins* cannot be forgiven until *we forgive.* The Bible says we must practice and learn how to forgive before we go to worship and pray. It's that important to God!

Jesus understood why the annual commanded days of corporate forgiveness were vital. He grew up watching the adults try to live it out. Maybe, during the month of Elul, just before Rosh Hashanah, he walked down the road as a boy with his father, visiting a neighbor who borrowed a tool and never returned it. He watched them as they agreed to a price and embraced each other in friendship.

God intends for us to clean out our closets from guilt or blame regularly, and requires His chosen community to search their minds and hearts to forgive. When the disciples asked, "How did you wither that tree with your word?" Jesus told them that forgiving all the time, not just one month a year, was a key to that power.

Do we then make void the law through faith? Certainly not! On the contrary, we establish the law.

Romans 3:31

Now, all these years later, far removed from commanded Holy Days in our Christian communities, we're immersed in errors caused by rejecting these directions. We need to understand the concept of forgiveness as a practical means to personal growth and a clear mandate from God. Our obedience to follow this command opens the way for huge spiritual strides. Then our words really mean something. When Christ forgives us, He expects us to imitate Him. As believers reach for the truth, we must submit to this circumcision of our hearts privately; then go further and share it with others in our community of faith, if we want to please God.

Paul bluntly told the church leaders who struggled with the diversity of the new people joining the congregation:

Receive one who is weak in the faith, *but* not to disputes over doubtful things.

Romans 14:1

Members of any particular congregation begin to develop spiritually when they forgive others for their differences. They bind together in the love of Jesus, the savior of people of every nation. Paul addressed the problems of blending Gentiles into Jewish congregations, encouraging them to focus on serving God with forgiving hearts, instead of judging and criticizing appearances.

One person esteems *one* day above another; another esteems every day *alike*. Let each be fully convinced in his own mind. He who observes the day, observes *it* to the Lord; and he who does not observe the day, to the Lord he does not observe *it*. He who eats, eats to the Lord, for he gives God thanks; and he who does not eat, to the Lord he does not eat, and gives God thanks. For none of us lives to himself, and no one dies to himself. For if we live, we live to the Lord; and if we die, we die to the Lord. Therefore, whether we live or die, we are the Lord's.

Romans 14:5-8

You may think that this passage seems out of place in a chapter that focuses on forgiveness. However, I believe that God calls us to re-examine our hearts to see how difficult we make it for each other, especially in our communities of faith. Jesus calls us to a ministry of discernment and loving reconciliation. When believers get stuck in a mindset where tradition or conformity takes the place of love, Jesus calls them out of the crowd saying, "Forgive them and follow me." We discover the wisdom in Jesus' example as we learn to discern and judge the spiritual content in our own lives and walk in the way of peace.

Notice His last instructions. When Jesus came back to the disciples after His resurrection, He summed up the laws of love and forgiveness:

"Peace to you! As the Father has sent Me, I also send you." And when He had said this, He breathed on *them*, and said to them again, "Receive the Holy Spirit. If you forgive the sins of any, they are forgiven them; if you retain the sins of any, they are retained."

John 20:21b-23

Do we live our lives as if we really understand the power we hold when we receive the Holy Spirit? Forgiving someone who sinned against us releases them from harsh judgment in the kingdom of God. This may not take away the consequences of their actions while they live on earth, but it opens the way for their own eternal peace.

In contrast, our condemnation of another person affects them, too. When we retain their sins and continue to blame them in our mind, two things occur: We put spiritual laws into motion which affect them, and by refusing to allow the Spirit to lead us we block our own blessing. We get tangled up in each other's spiritual wellbeing until we forgive and are forgiven.

Our opportunity to set someone free from their sins with forgiveness sounds strange to us, but Jesus told us to do it when we receive His Spirit. Such action requires faith in the unseen activity of God. This is the stuff that healing is made of. This kind of love transforms impossible despair into enduring peace and joy as it emanates from the Spirit of Christ. We simply share it. This kind of love protects us from all bitterness or sense of unfairness.

Then Jesus said, "Father, forgive them, for they do not know what they do."

Luke 23:34

Imagine Jesus, just about to enter the realm of death. He harbored no resentment for His bad treatment and released all men from the errors of hateful and self-serving natures. His forgiving Spirit loves others in a way that we could never love them on our own. He offers this same Spirit to all men, regardless of their past, when they believe.

Jesus prayed, **"And forgive us our debts, as we forgive our debtors. And do not lead us into temptation, but deliver us from the evil one."**

Matthew 6:12-13a

God forgives us to the same degree that we forgive others. He calls us to examine our own interaction with people to understand how it works. We demonstrate His generosity when we pour out forgiveness for each other. Then He fills us to overflowing again.

Turn the Other Cheek

When you read the words of Christ and they don't make any sense, you know they need special consideration and time. Dig into the following concepts and ask Jesus to show you a deep spiritual truth today. If you disagree or look for a rational explanation of His message, that's okay, as long as you seek His wisdom and talk to Him directly with an inquiring mind. If you find yourself feeling adversarial or defensive about the text, it's possible that God's word hit a raw nerve. Thank Him for pointing it out to you. Pray specifically about sensitivity to a repellent doctrine until your heart fully listens to Him and you receive a precision healing in your life.

Jesus sat upon a mountainside teaching. You can hear His desire for our lives to be blessed for eternity. He connected several important repellent doctrines together, the most famous and misunderstood: "**turn the other cheek**". Listen as He pours out the mind of God and turns everything worldly upside down:

> **Blessed are you when they revile and persecute you, and say all kinds of evil against you falsely for My sake. Rejoice and be exceedingly glad, for great *is* your reward in heaven, for so they persecuted the prophets who were before you.**
>
> **Matthew 5:11**

Around the globe we know that the people of God suffer the consequences of standing in faith. In Christian nations, the worst that we contend with is ridicule for our beliefs. Scripture tells us to prepare for harsh treatment and know how to respond in the face of insult and even threat of death, as if that day may come in our lifetime. Learn God's word and make yourself useful for the kingdom. It takes courage to stand for the truth when people mock you, but Jesus gives you a secret to the kingdom: enjoy the challenge! Be yourself and don't let others sway you from your purpose.

You are the salt of the earth; but if the salt loses its flavor, how shall it be seasoned? It is then good for nothing but to be thrown out and trampled underfoot by men.

Matthew 5:13

God wants to preserve our uniqueness, tenderize our hearts and flavor our lives. If we become pretentious people who feign righteousness, we cover up qualities that He gave us on purpose. He uses our flaws as great tools for the kingdom. With honest straight talk about our lives thus far, we connect in a meaningful way to bring people to Him and keep our zest for living. Then we light the way for others to follow by example.

You are the light of the world. A city that is set on a hill cannot be hidden. Nor do they light a lamp and put it under a basket, but on a lampstand, and it gives light to all *who are* in the house.

Matthew 5:14-15

Find the hidden meaning. Sometimes we're like torches seen from a distance, burning with compassion. We're on fire with enthusiasm to share His love. We'll tell the world that God adopted us when we found it impossible to cope without Him. Yet within our own "house" we need to shine the lamp to expose the unclean spirits that love darkness. They cannot tolerate His light. Let John clarify this further before we go on.

This is the message which we have heard from Him and declare to you, that God is light and in Him is no darkness at all. If we say that we have fellowship with Him, and walk in darkness, we lie and do not practice the truth.

1 John 1:5-6

Darkness provides cover for lies and deception. We often look for other people's opinions instead of moving toward the light and following God. Walking in the light of Christ prepares us for fellowship with our Father in the kingdom of heaven within us.

A believer's ongoing experience with Christ goes like this when we learn to use the light of truth: The Holy Spirit **intercedes** for us, **teaches us**, **confirms the truth**, and **speaks God's words** to us. Members of God's family discern between good and evil as part of our spiritual identity. When deception enters our thoughts, we shine a light on it. The Holy Spirit sends the evil inclination away, but it will try to come back again. Angels stand guard with us while we learn to use our righteous defenses in the kingdom. All this takes place during our time on earth. Once we begin to master this kind of righteousness, God's light will shine *through* us. People will see it from a distance! That's fellowship with Him! Now go back to Matthew:

Let your light so shine before men, that they may see your good works and glorify your Father in heaven. Do not think that I came to destroy the Law or the Prophets. I did not come to destroy but to fulfill.

Matthew 5:16-17

Jesus put His thoughts together exactly as God spoke them, always placing special emphasis on His Law. Your light shines for others when Christ's Spirit works in you to fulfill His Law. Believers must wonder how our faith moved so far away from faithful Israelites who loved God's laws and strived for holiness. They kept the word of God for thousands of years before Christ came to earth. I don't know if any of my ancestors came from one of the twelve tribes of Israel. Most people don't know. But as adopted members of the family of Abraham, we set ourselves apart as light-bearers and word-carriers for all nations. Many faithful Torah-keeping Jews love God wholeheartedly, yet seem to have scales over their eyes concerning the Messiah who turned our world upside down. Christians often have scales over their eyes regarding God's love for His chosen people. He unites us in His purpose. Jesus explains how His Light and God's Law connect seamlessly.

Whoever therefore breaks one of the least of these commandments, and teaches men so, shall be called least in the kingdom of heaven; but whoever does and teaches *them*, he shall be called great in the kingdom of heaven. For I say to you, that unless your righteousness exceeds *the righteousness* of the scribes and Pharisees, you will by no means enter the kingdom of heaven.

Matthew 5:19-20

I want to be called great for all eternity, don't you? The Pharisees sang the entire Torah from memory, and we struggle to memorize a few verses. The scribes often labored more than a year to complete a Torah scroll. With such scriptural knowledge, you'd think they would have been the most righteous of all! The corruption of the physical world rendered many of them ineffective, despite their vast intelligence and careful observation of the Law. They believed *in* God, no doubt. They followed all of the religious rules. Yet they could not enter the kingdom.

What about you and me? Does our physical world render us useless, or will we be called great for all eternity? In our churches today, we see people who use the knowledge of scripture and try to follow it to the letter; yet they cannot actually hear God anymore. Maybe their hearts hardened around a doctrine or tradition. If they fail to act with love in their hearts, He provides lessons of correction and discipline.

Let's all begin to move together toward Christ Himself. Our God is not a religion or a set of laws, yet keeping His commands brings reward in the spiritual hierarchy of heaven. Know them. Practice them. Don't choose greatness on earth as your goal, but take up the march toward eternal power and authority as a humble servant while you're here. I suspect that we've misunderstood this, so take a look again at these words: **"Whoever therefore breaks one of the least of these commandments, and teaches men so, shall be called least in the kingdom of heaven; but whoever does and teaches *them,* he shall be called great in the kingdom of heaven."** Begin to seek God's own heart to understand His laws better. He allows us to join Him as He extends His love and grace. Jesus expects far more from us now than the Pharisees who obeyed God's laws to the letter without love in their hearts.

> **You have heard that it was said to those of old, *'You shall not murder,* and whoever murders will be in danger of the judgment.'** **But I say to you that whoever is angry with his brother without a cause shall be in danger of the judgment. And whoever says to his brother, 'Raca!' shall be in danger of the council. But whoever says, 'You fool!' shall be in danger of hell fire.**
> **Matthew 5:21-22**

Christ points to the power of your thoughts and cautions that that your own words can bring judgment upon you. Make sure you check your anger and test it against God's truth. By losing your temper and letting words fly out of your mouth to hurt someone, you create a dangerous environment in the spirit. If you condemn others who struggle with the flesh, Jesus warns that this attitude leads *you* to "dead" works and puts you in grave spiritual peril. The Adversary needs no permission to hassle you because you left the door wide open and invited him into your spirit by refusing to control this inclination. The misery, or judgment, we bring upon ourselves and others can be traced to a loose tongue, a prideful heart or a sour outlook, and our ability to serve God is tied to our willingness to adjust these areas.

> **Therefore if you bring your gift to the altar, and there remember that your brother has something against you, leave your gift there before the altar, and go your way. First be reconciled to your brother, and then come and offer your gift.**
> **Matthew 5:23-24**

Now slow down and read that again. If someone has something against you, that's their problem, right? Not according to Jesus. When we leave disputes, disagreements, or misunderstandings unattended, our sacrifice, *our service to the Lord*, must halt until we settle the matter. This reference to *brother* indicates that we must give special notice to our brothers and sisters in our community of faith. If you had squabbles or misunderstandings in your church, how did your community handle it? Did people get mad and leave the church? I grieve over the condition of our lukewarm churches and continue to pray that the truth will bind us all together to please God and obey His commands.

> **Agree with your adversary quickly, while you are on the way with him, lest your adversary deliver you to the judge, the judge hand you over to the officer, and you be thrown into prison. Assuredly, I say to you, you will by no means get out of there till you have paid the last penny.**
>
> **Matthew 5:25-26**

We live in a world of lawsuits, complaints and disputes. Jesus cautions us to settle our disagreements with each other before it goes too far. Some people spend their energy blaming others, not wanting to face their own error in a dispute. Jesus warns us that we could find ourselves indebted- even imprisoned- by refusing to repent of such attitudes, bringing judgment upon ourselves. Whether we owe a debt or an apology, we need to settle up for our own good.

SPIRITUAL ADVERSARIES TEST US.

Pause here now, and squeeze deeper meaning out of this passage. Jesus hints at the freedom of children of God when they learn to deal with their spiritual adversaries effectively. When we approach our spiritual opponent to resolve a matter, we learn how to keep cool next time we're under spiritual attack. However, if we ignore our spiritual enemy and make no effort to control our flesh, then the demonic adversaries gain the upper hand and leave us with few choices. God allows spiritual adversaries to coordinate attacks on our weaknesses so that we will not just drift along. He designed them to get our attention, try us, and push us hard enough to develop spiritual strength. Work through these lessons quickly and get your certificate of achievement in the kingdom of heaven. Go on to the next test. Don't get stuck learning the same lesson all your life, as most of us do, and end up imprisoned by your inability to deal with it effectively. Get on the right side of His Law and make amends. Settle it, once and for all, before you stand in front of the judge.

> **You have heard that it was said to those of old, *'You shall not commit adultery.'* But I say to you that whoever looks at a woman to lust for her has already committed adultery with her in his heart. If your right eye causes you to sin, pluck it out and cast it from you.**
>
> **Matthew 5:27-28a**

We are told to examine our own hearts, identify our sins, and take swift, decisive action to avoid compromising with silent sins in our thoughts. Jesus, talking to Jews, assumed their knowledge of the laws regarding adultery (punishable by death). He issued this directive regarding the serious sins of bad intentions such as lust: Go to any extreme to get rid of them forever. We could spend hours discussing this part and trying to explain it away, but keep reading. It gets even more intense.

> **You have heard that it was said, *'An eye for an eye and a tooth for a tooth.'* But I tell you not to resist an evil person. But whoever slaps you on your right cheek, turn the other to him also. If anyone wants to sue you and take away your tunic, let him have *your* cloak also. And whoever compels you to go one mile, go with him two. Give to him who asks you, and from him who wants to borrow from you do not turn away.**
>
> **Matthew 5:38-42**

Wrapped between arguments against getting even with evil people and graphic lessons on generosity, we see the famous phrase about turning the other cheek. Read it several times. Hear Him telling us to look at the spiritual side of every situation instead of the physical circumstance. How much do we know about the problems of the person who just offended us? Have we considered their spiritual condition? Did God send them to test us? Our Creator calls us to embrace this radical thinking as we practice love in response to daily challenges.

> **You have heard that it was said, *'You shall love your neighbor* and hate your enemy.' But I say to you, love your enemies, bless those who curse you, do good to those who hate you, and pray for those who spitefully use you and persecute you, that you may be sons of your Father in heaven; for He makes His sun rise on the evil and on the good, and sends rain on the just and on the unjust. For if you love those who love you, what reward have you? Do not even the tax collectors do the same? And if you greet your brethren only, what do you do more *than others?* Do not even the tax collectors do so? Therefore you shall be perfect, just as your Father in heaven is perfect.**
>
> **Matthew 5:43-48**

When you begin to obey Jesus with these things in mind, Satan will throw a fit. He will fill you with anguish and whisper his familiar words. *"You know your weaknesses. You can't be perfect like your Father. You can't take these things literally."* Or he might just keep reminding you of other people's sins and say, *"You'll forgive but you'll never forget."* He won't give up easily. When you start to deal with the real meaning of the words of Jesus instead of debating about them or yawning through the familiar text, the power of the Holy Spirit activates in you to overcome the devil.

The keys to the kingdom and power in such spiritual encounters hang on the repellent ideas in this passage. **Look for a way to love your enemy.** When you find yourself doing that, Love Himself covers all mistakes and lights the way.

The mouth of the righteous is a well of life, but violence covers the mouth of the wicked. Hatred stirs up strife, but love covers all sins.

Proverbs 10:11-12

Your path to reconciliation lies in a region that Satan defends vigorously. You'll find plenty of people under his influence as the wicked stir up violence and despair. Until you are fully equipped for battle, rely on faith in Jesus to defeat the opposition. In spiritual warfare, you'll learn to be creative as you practice. If you feel angry, focus your fury on those spirits that tried to take you captive. Get out your spiritual duct tape and see yourself binding those demons of regret and blame together so they can't function. Leave them out on your spiritual wall as a warning to the spirits of argument and resentment not to mess with you anymore. Sound the trumpets. Let them know you're declaring war on them. Allow Love to stimulate a new vision of purpose. Know your rights in the kingdom. Take control of your thoughts and words and cooperate with the Spirit of Christ when He teaches you how to overcome hatred with love.

When something terrible happens, don't despair! Jesus turns everything upside down and wrong-side out! We have strength in the spiritual realm that *appears* passive in our world.

Who is wise and understanding among you? Let him show by good conduct that his works are done in the meekness of wisdom.

James 3:13

Righteous people appear humble in their conduct, while in the spirit they're overpowering demons in the kingdom. Your willingness to apply this mysterious truth every day is anything but passive, but instead of worldly fame, you reflect God's glory. This same humility, this willingness to yield to Him, empowers you to replace your own ego, full of hot air, with the breath of God, His own powerful Spirit. Instead of venting anger toward a person who seems to oppose you, demolish the underlying spirits who strike at the foundations of your path of peace.

The humility of Christ clears out pride to cultivate godlike personality traits in us. The humility of Christ sees past the sin all the way to forgiveness. Instead of tearing people down or dominating them with our ideas, we find ways to help them fit into the body of Christ. While earthbound we may feel overwhelmed or distracted, but listen for our Father's voice. He said to go the extra mile with a persistent commitment to alter the lives of people we touch. Not just any kind of service will do, because God judges our intent before He promotes us in the kingdom. If we try to serve others with our own purpose in mind, or seek *any* glory, then it smacks of wrong motives.

Begin to *see* your spiritual battles. The same God who told the Israelites destroy everyone and take no captives when they conquered the Canaanites often urges us to turn the other cheek. It's not an earthly fight. He hates evil, treachery and abuse. He tells us to command principalities and powers in the spiritual kingdom, and expects us to take no prisoners when we rid ourselves of defiant spirits!

When confronted by the devil, Jesus resisted with robust knowledge of scripture. He walked calmly alongside evil without any need to fight or flee. He understands our struggles and fears, but leads the way for us to take our place as kings and priests with authority over Satan, too. Instead of practicing pacifism that borders on cowardice or ignorance of spiritual truths, we need to arm ourselves with the word, a sharp two-edged sword. Jesus taught us to proactively love sinners even as they sin against us, a seemingly impossible task if not for His indwelling Spirit. When it comes to minor insults and ignorance, we should waste no time or energy fighting back.

When Jesus stood before Pilate, who asked, "What have you done?" He simply answered:

My kingdom is not of this world. If My kingdom were of this world, My servants would fight, so that I should not be delivered to the Jews; but now My kingdom is not from here.

John 18:36

121

Jesus reminds us that we are not of this world. He insists that we use our situation to reflect a peace that surpasses understanding, and show wisdom regarding all trivial matters.

If someone hurts you, you may instinctively react with a desire to get back at them. *"How could they do this to me?"* That's natural. But as a child of God, pause for a moment and raise yourself from the natural to the supernatural. Push aside those angry words and prideful feelings. No, on second thought, throw them back in the face of that spirit of pride and push him into the abyss. Disarm the spirits of ungodly fear and put them to death. Identify your spiritual foes, look for them in your kingdom and overcome them with God's own words. Forgive the person who offended you. Rise up and take a step to change your life... a change in your thinking...

Remember that other people possess weakness and flaws, and Jesus died for them, too. Maybe He put them in your life so you can practice giving His kind of extraordinary love, expecting nothing in return. God desires healing in our relationships. He lifts us above the sorrow of any abuse to find the hope of truth. Jesus cleanses the wound of that situation when we turn to Him in earnest. Trust that He works for the good for those who love Him.

Please do not take these words out of context. Physical or mental abuse in a relationship should motivate the recipient to change something. If danger threatens, Jesus does not oblige us to foolishly sit by and do nothing. Begin with a prayer and turn the whole situation over to Him. If He tells you to get going, don't just sit there praying about it! You may need to move on. He supplies the only hope of reconciliation through His sacrifice on the cross. God uses the hands and feet of His believers to provide support and encouragement. Ask Him to send wise counsel. Get out of harm's way as soon as possible and begin the process that leads to forgiveness.

When the emotional healing begins, remember that God loves passionate people. He knows that hitting bottom ignites a powerful catalyst for change, and He harnesses a broken life for His good purpose. Like a wild horse, God can take your strong will and bridle it to give you a sense of direction.

When abusive people confronted Jesus, He took a unique approach.

When they hurled their insults at Him, He did not retaliate; when He suffered, He made no threats. Instead, He entrusted Himself to Him who judges justly.

1 Peter 2:23 (NIV)

God Himself has set an example for us. In this world, abuse rears its ugly head far too often. Trust Him to deal with the offenders.[54] Our obedience to Him aligns us with His power and truth, regardless of the appearance. When Christ takes over in someone's life, the hope of change becomes a guarantee. In His supreme love for us, Jesus exemplified victory over abuse, whether physical or verbal. We don't need the last word in a dispute with man to be right with God, but we do need to get our mind and heart right.

Confusion about "turning the other cheek" lulls Christians into huge omissions in the spiritual world and renders them ineffective in the physical world around them. When Jesus spoke these words, a slap on the cheek meant insult, not physical assault. Jesus Himself displayed anger when He perceived fakes and liars. He passionately protested dishonesty and loudly rebuked religious hypocrites. His sacrifice opened the way to complete healing and absolute peace. He showed us how to live life in victory, even when it appears that we are victims. An unfair relationship can bring out something greater in us if we apply these principles.

Jesus exemplified the process of physically backing down, of turning the other cheek, of complete surrender to God's will. It takes more courage than fighting back. As He hung from the cross, Jesus' love spoke through the pain when He asked His Father to forgive the people who came against Him. He knew that they did not fully understand what they were doing. His Spirit, our Counselor, empowers us with such a love.

---

54   Romans 12:1-21,Leviticus 19:15-18, Nahum 1:2-3,Romans 2:1-16, Ezekiel 33:31

SPIRITUAL INERTIA

Our thoughts tend to go like this: "Someday when things are more perfect...someday when the right person comes along... someday when we have more money...maybe when we have more time..." We keep buying things and re-arranging our physical surroundings to stay happy. We concentrate on how we look, the health of our bodies, what we eat, where we live, what kind of a mood we are in... on and on in pursuit of a good life on earth. But eventually, we get to a point where we're stuck. Hard decisions, difficult circumstances, or a nagging feeling that we've missed something.... God uses these to draw us closer to Him.

Jesus guarantees to change your life as He spends time with you personally.

> **But the Helper, the Holy Spirit, whom the Father will send in My name, He will teach you all things, and bring to your remembrance all things that I said to you. Peace I leave with you, My peace I give to you; not as the world gives do I give to you. Let not your heart be troubled, neither let it be afraid.**
>
> **John 14:26-27**

For now, God makes no promises about the absence of war or the kind of peace we hear about on the news. His lasting peace holds us steady when everything seems to go wrong. It allows us to see our life from a larger perspective. When fear of losing anything on earth overcomes you, learn to recognize the spiritual enemy who tries to hold you spellbound. If the spirits of fear create the illusion that the world is closing in on you, you'll feel like a victim, trapped in your own circumstances or lost in your mistakes. There you fall to your knees and call out for help from your rich and powerful Father who rules the universe.

You didn't want to bother Him again. After all, you really believed in self reliance. Prepare yourself for a great adventure when you finally turn your anguish over to Him and cry out, "This would be impossible without You, Lord. I believe that You will protect me if I obey You."

The angels have watched and waited for this moment. For God, it represents the perfect time to extend His grace. For you, it may feel like the worst time in your life, but God knows the end of the story. Rejoice when you get to this repellent place in your journey! Hitting bottom quickens your response to His call and readies you for action. It's the reoccurring theme of scripture.

Let's look back at the story of the Israelites again, just freed from their slavery in Egypt. God had sent horrendous plagues upon the Pharaoh to convince him that he must release the Jews. In the last plague, the Egyptian firstborn sons died; the grieving Pharaoh told them to leave the area and take their powerful God with them. Imagine thousands evacuating. Quickly they gathered their families and belongings and followed Moses out of the city. Miles away from town, they stopped by the sea. They might have taken a better route, but they followed God's instructions.

Now the LORD spoke to Moses, saying: "Speak to the children of Israel, that they turn ... by the sea. For Pharaoh will say of the children of Israel, 'They *are* bewildered by the land; the wilderness has closed them in.' Then I will harden Pharaoh's heart, so that he will pursue them; and I will gain honor over

Pharaoh and over all his army, that the Egyptians may know that I *am* the LORD." And they did so.

Exodus 14:1-4

Don't miss the way God used Pharaoh's stubbornness in this story. All the men in his army could see that there was no way out for the Israelites. Our mishaps serve to prove His greatness, *not ours*, when we join Him.

Now it was told the king of Egypt that the people had fled, and the heart of Pharaoh and his servants was turned against the people; and they said, "Why have we done this, that we have let Israel go from serving us?" So he made ready his chariot and took his people with him. Also, he took six hundred choice chariots, and all the chariots of Egypt with captains over every one of them.

Exodus 14:5-7

Does the pharaoh symbolize a stubborn and unyielding influence in your spiritual life? His power over the Israelites kept them in unquestionable bondage for years.

And when Pharaoh drew near, the children of Israel lifted their eyes, and behold, the Egyptians marched after them.

Exodus 14:10a

The Israelites had grown accustomed to their life as slaves. They carried few weapons and felt vulnerable out in the desert. They stood watching in horror, backs against beaches of the Red Sea, as that terrifying cloud of stomping horses and men with clattering swords rushed toward them.

So they were very afraid, and the children of Israel cried out to the LORD. Then they said to Moses, "Because *there were* no graves in Egypt, have you taken us away to die in the wilderness? Why have you so dealt with us, to bring us up out of Egypt? *Is* this not the word that we told you in Egypt,

126

saying, 'Let us alone that we may serve the Egyptians'? For *it would have been* better for us to serve the Egyptians than that we should die in the wilderness."

Exodus 14:10b-12

Listen for the complaining and doubting. A slave mentality causes you to look only at the physical side of your problem and ignore the greater vision of God's purpose. Ungodly negative spirits go straight to the minds and hearts of the people they invade. Then they try to take over the tongue. Here's one of the reasons God operates in groups of people. People of faith need each other so that when they feel weak and vulnerable, someone will hear God speaking His truth and remind the others. At this pivotal moment in history, the Israelites listened to their prophet as God spoke to them all.

And Moses said to the people, "Do not be afraid. Stand still, and see the salvation of the LORD, which He will accomplish for you today. For the Egyptians whom you see today, you shall see again no more forever. The LORD will fight for you, and you shall hold your peace."

Exodus 14:13-14

A key to the kingdom lies right here in this action adventure! Stand still in the middle of your disaster, claim the calm that God promises and regain your composure as a child of God. First, and most importantly, you need to see *the salvation of the LORD*! When we get in a bad situation and want God to save us, we must see it in the spiritual kingdom before we can see it in the physical. Then listen for instructions. The spiritually mature among us hear Him when He speaks during a crisis and follow His directions. That's faith. Now look at the very next verse:

And the LORD said to Moses, "Why do you cry to Me? Tell the children of Israel to go forward."

Exodus 14:15

At first they stood frozen in their tracks, terror stricken as they watched the army coming toward them. They cried about the unfairness of it all. Totally unprepared for a fight, they knew they had no choice except to trust God's ridiculous instructions. So, despite the appearances, they hastily packed again and walked right into the water *before* Moses raised his staff and parted the sea. The obedient action came first. *Then* God moved the water so the Israelites could cross over to a new life.

How often do we pray, "God, will you help me with this problem?" and then wait for Him to rearrange our circumstances before we follow His instructions? The Israelites' obedience *preceded* God's intervention for them in the crisis. I'm convinced the leaders took Moses' word for it and stepped out in faith while Moses listened to detailed directions:

> **But lift up your rod, and stretch out your hand over the sea and divide it. And the children of Israel shall go on dry *ground* through the midst of the sea. And I indeed will harden the hearts of the Egyptians, and they shall follow them. So I will gain honor over Pharaoh and over all his army, his chariots, and his horsemen. Then the Egyptians shall know that I *am* the LORD, when I have gained honor for Myself over Pharaoh, his chariots, and his horsemen.**
>
> **Exodus 14:16-18**

There's something else here that we often overlook. When I meditated about this passage, I realized that God uses *our obedience* to reveal Himself to *our enemies*. He uses our worst predicaments to demonstrate His power in our lives for all to see. Do you wonder if some of those Egyptians who died when the sea crashed over them will stand before God as believers in heaven? Do we frustrate God with our disobedience and cowardice when He plans to show His power to our enemies?

> **And the Angel of God, who went before the camp of Israel, moved and went behind them; and the pillar of cloud went from before them and stood behind them. So it came between**

the camp of the Egyptians and the camp of Israel. Thus it was a cloud and darkness *to the one,* and it gave light by night *to the other,* so that the one did not come near the other all that night.

Exodus 14:19-20

I often marvel over the invisible protection that surely surrounds me during my darkest hours. Just like the Israelites, when our spiritual enemies pursue us, God protects His family. He obstructs the enemy's vision and keeps us from seeing danger when we look back; but moving forward, He lights the way!

Then Moses stretched out his hand over the sea; and the LORD caused the sea to go *back* by a strong east wind all that night, and made the sea into dry *land,* and the waters were divided. So the children of Israel went into the midst of the sea on the dry *ground,* and the waters *were* a wall to them on their right hand and on their left.

Exodus 14:21-22

God physically intervenes when we need Him the most. This message of hope stands specifically for those who put one foot in front of the other against all sound reasoning and follow His instructions.

And the Egyptians pursued and went after them into the midst of the sea, all Pharaoh's horses, his chariots, and his horsemen. Now it came to pass, in the morning watch, that the LORD looked down upon the army of the Egyptians through the pillar of fire and cloud, and He troubled the army of the Egyptians. And He took off their chariot wheels, so that they drove them with difficulty; and the Egyptians said, "Let us flee from the face of Israel, for the LORD fights for them against the Egyptians." Then the LORD said to Moses, "Stretch out your hand over the sea, that the waters may come back upon

the Egyptians, on their chariots, and on their horsemen."
And Moses stretched out his hand over the sea; and when the
morning appeared, the sea returned to its full depth, while the
Egyptians were fleeing into it. So the LORD overthrew the
Egyptians in the midst of the sea. Then the waters returned
and covered the chariots, the horsemen, *and* all the army of
Pharaoh that came into the sea after them. Not so much as one
of them remained.

But the Israelites went through the sea on dry ground, with
a wall of water on their right and on their left. That day the
LORD saved Israel from the hands of the Egyptians, and
Israel saw the Egyptians lying dead on the shore. And when
the Israelites saw the great power the LORD displayed against
the Egyptians, the people feared the LORD and put their trust
in Him and in Moses His servant.

Exodus 14:23-31

This great story illustrates God's intervention for His people when
they obey Him. It leaps out as a tale of God's power over the physical
world we live in. The subtle truth of such intercession reveals itself in one
assertive step of faith into the water *before* He parts our sea.

I wonder if He set wonderful possibilities in motion long ago and
waits for us to trigger our own miracles. Our stubborn refusal to trust Him
to part our sea leaves us standing in this world waiting to take the first step.
When we choose to criticize, blame or make excuses about a situation, our
spiritual inertia blocks God's intercession. It keeps us in bondage. *"If only
we had time to build rafts..."* they might have reasoned.

We find parts of ourselves all over this story. Sometimes we represent
the pharaoh, trying to hold power over someone when it rightfully belongs
to God. Sometimes we get stuck, complaining and wishing for better days.
And sometimes we step out in faith and everyone sees God in action. Obey
Him immediately when you hear His voice. He wants you to do something
that would be impossible for you to do without Him.

At the onset of a crisis, He tells us to stand firm and be still. Stop whatever you usually do and ask God for guidance. Remember, if you begin to hear negative chatter in your head, you need to take your mind off of the pharaoh and the bondage. Choose to hear God's voice. Turn you mind to the impossible situation before you and take a mental step into it. Then another.

Imagine that as you keep going, the water recedes with each step until you get to the other side. Now sit down on the bank and look back at your problem from the grassy slope. You cannot see it in the same way, ever again, because your obedience to trust God changed your perspective. Other people will see you there on the other side. Your story will encourage them to a greater faith in our huge God.

Ask Christ's Spirit to reveal the ideas that pursue you and enslave you. This time, as they come to mind, instead of looking back with fear and dread, allow Him to cloud your vision about your problems as you turn away from them. Let the sea crash over them behind you. Move forward with complete assurance that God pays attention to the requests of His faithful children!

The Israelites endured a long night, but at daybreak they saw the result of their obedience. If they had surrendered in a panic or hesitated at the edge of the water any longer, the Egyptians would have captured them again.

Is God constantly planning such drama in our lives? Are we missing something huge while we complain about our situation and submit a list of "if-only" options to Him? When children of God try to operate on their own courage and self-reliance, they miss His purpose and get stranded in one place. Millions of people trudge through life, believing they are slaves to sin, when God intended victory for them. Has pride hardened our hearts? Have we allowed our doubts and double-mindedness to consume us? Break free and travel into the grand adventure waiting for you right at the muddy banks of your own unapproachable Red Sea.

Your Creator has it all planned out. He's encouraging us to move on through the night together so that at daybreak we can say, "Wow! Look what God has done!"

THE HOPE OF CHANGE

Instead of getting discouraged about the changes you need to make, I trust that you will find hope in God's word. He enables you with the power of the Holy Spirit to deal with the demons that test you. When you pass a test, you'll feel hopeful because you're learning to use God's spiritual tools. This, in turn, gives you a sense of balance and purpose about your own circumstances.

Jesus explained it to Peter and the disciples.

> **And I will give you the keys of the kingdom of heaven, and whatever you bind on earth will be bound in heaven, and whatever you loose on earth will be loosed in heaven.**
>
> **Matthew 16:19**

Our Father allows us to use a process often translated "binding" in the King James version. The Hebrew language conveys some rich concepts within the words, and we gain new insight by looking at these different meanings in the word "bind".

The Hebrew word, **"acar"**[55] means **"to tie, bind, imprison, harness,**

55   Strong's H631, Condensed Brown-Driver-Briggs Hebrew Lexicon, Thayer's Greek Lexicon

to gird, to begin the battle, make the attack, of obligation of oath, to be imprisoned, bound to be taken prisoner."

In the following Old Testament verse, explore a foundational law of God. Our words affect our own wellbeing, and represent a common stumbling block for many people. Yet this same truth gives us reason for hope when we apply the knowledge and skill of a child of God. Children of God practice by speaking the words of their Father and removing the expressions that go against the kingdom. God's language only works for good, not evil. As we grow, we learn to faithfully handle such a force behind our words, not wanting to waste our breath on useless talk.

If a man makes a vow to the LORD or swears an oath to bind himself by some agreement, he shall not break his word; he shall do according to all that proceeds out of his mouth.

Numbers 30:1b-2

Your words bind you in the spirit, whether you realize it or not, according to God's law. You think they simply disappear into the air, but God put His breath in you. If you're part of His family, when His breath passes through your lips, your words carry authority. If you consistently ignore this, God considers it sinful; you become entangled in the consequences of your own failure to control them. But if you learn to apply His purpose to your words, you hold power beyond your understanding. Your words carry the power to bring good - or misery that leads to repentance - based on the intent behind them!

God knows if He can entrust His authority to you by the words you speak. Until you use them to build the kingdom, you remain immature in the spirit as a child of God. You may actually become a **prisoner** of the consequences of your own words if you allow them to run wild. But the moment you decide to practice using your words wisely, you start to see exciting results in your life. In the beginning, you may struggle with old habits, reactions and patterns of speech; but at some point, God sees that He can consistently trust your words. Then He gives them the full force of His Spirit.

When you pass that test, you become a powerful opponent against the devil. Now look back at some of the other meanings listed above and apply them to your spiritual battles to overcome a problem. Imagine how you could **harness** your words for the kingdom of God. Begin a spiritual **battle** to overcome unclean spirits. Use them to **attack** the adversary.

Now look at another Hebrew word translated as "bind": **"chabash**[56]**: to tie, bind, bind on, bind up, saddle, restrain, bandage, govern".**

> **The Spirit of the Lord GOD is upon Me, because the LORD has anointed Me to preach good tidings to the poor; He has sent Me to heal** (chabash) **the brokenhearted, to proclaim liberty to the captives, and the opening of the prison to those who are bound** (acar) **...**
>
> **Isaiah 61:1.**

This verse uses both Hebrew words for bind, and gives rich insight into the mind of God. You find the word "chabash", sometimes translated as "heal or bind" (bandage) the brokenhearted, and the word "acar" (imprisoned) also appears later. Can you see the call to servant-hood in this message? Not only shall you bind demons, but offer freedom and healing to all who suffer under their oppression (including you).

When Jesus reconciles you to the Father and cleans you up to come into the family, He teaches you what you need to know. When unclean spirits come against you, take the opportunity to practice what you learn. These tests allow God to see if you're serious about keeping His law. Instead of feeling sorry for yourself because you experience new challenges, literally quit giving a place to these unclean thoughts, so they must leave or die. If they try to return, stand firm against them before they get too far. Acquire increasing authority in overcoming them, and take your inherited place with His sons and daughters so that:

> **... the God of our Lord Jesus Christ, the Father of glory, may give to you the spirit of wisdom and revelation in the knowledge**

---

56   Strong's H2280, Condensed Brown-Driver-Briggs Hebrew Lexicon, Thayer's Greek Lexicon

of Him, the eyes of your understanding being enlightened; that you may know what is the hope of His calling, what are the riches of the glory of His inheritance in the saints, and what is the exceeding greatness of His power toward us who believe, according to the working of His mighty power which He worked in Christ when He raised Him from the dead and seated Him at His right hand in the heavenly places, far above all principality and power and might and dominion, and every name that is named, not only in this age, but also in that which is to come.

Ephesians 1:17-21

When you pay attention to the spiritual side of everything, you make yourself available to God. Our inheritance on earth and throughout eternity involves just such powerful interaction. Whatever the circumstance, He'll use you if you listen and follow. Whether you feel like you've been knocked flat by bad luck or do not have what it takes to keep going in hard times, God's strength prevails. Of course, you must choose to use the tools He's given you so far. He waits for you to join Him.

You learn to display the humility and love befitting a child of God every time you face an opposing point of view. (Our Father is kind to the unthankful and evil.)[57] You learn to recognize the spirits opposing His kingdom, but treat the people they occupy with mercy.

This way of life provides renewed hope for real change. In your own walk, a peace-filled spirit replaces arrogant defiance and diffuses explosive arguments. If one person refuses to participate in a quarrel, then the other party cannot keep the battle going alone. It marks the beginning of a shift in communication with a loved one or an enemy.[58] When you practice righteousness, you possess a shield that keeps the fiery darts of the devil from hurting you with words.

---

57   Luke 6:35
58   James 3:2-10

**And the tongue is a fire, a world of iniquity. The tongue is so
set among our members that it defiles the whole body, and sets
on fire the course of nature; and it is set on fire by hell.**

James 3:6

Use your words wisely. Day by day, you gently practice and assist
others entangled in sin by filtering your words through love before you
speak.[59] When you set your mind on God's everlasting purpose, you
discover your Christ-centered identity. However, if you continue to
identify more with things of the world, your ego may try to stop you from
following this important imperative:

**Bless those who persecute you; bless and do not curse. Rejoice
with those who rejoice, and weep with those who weep. Be of
the same mind toward one another. Do not set your mind on
high things, but associate with the humble. Do not be wise in
your own opinion.**

Romans 12:14-16

I urge you to concentrate on Paul's words for a moment, because we
stand dangerously close to the fiery pit at this point. Twice we're told to
go further and bless someone when they persecute us. I know of very
few Christians who practice this basic principle of spiritual warfare. They
try not to curse their enemy with their mouth, but bless them under the
circumstances- never! You see, we spend most of our time thinking of the
flesh, the physical. Remember your identity in Christ. Strangers on earth,[60]
chosen to show the face of Love, we need to **pray for our enemies** and be
of the **same mind toward one another**.

Such knowledge of the kingdom proves deadly to spirits coming
against you. When you follow God's voice and try to say and do exactly
what you hear our Father say, two things happen. You overcome the devil,
and people get a genuine glimpse of God's peace-filled spirit working in

---

59   The context of James 3 is a warning to those who teach God's word. Self seeking and bitter
      envy in those who spread the gospel indicate that they carry demonic spirits.
60   Hebrews 11:13

His servant. I don't pretend to understand it, but the Spirit of Truth, like a personal trainer, exercises us in the exact target areas we need to work on. If we feel unlucky in an area of life, He'll graciously give us opportunities to apply His wisdom to change our thinking.

For example, if you get stuck in a cycle of lack, share what He's given you and overcome the devil by demonstrating the generosity of God. If you need anything on earth, God is your source. He expects you to exhibit good stewardship, but real blessings revolve around a close walk with the Father to learn His ways. Nothing else really matters. We see tangible results from our practice of binding when we get past our painful mistake patterns and overcome them.

> **Now no chastening seems to be joyful for the present, but painful; nevertheless, afterward it yields the peaceable fruit of righteousness to those who have been trained by it. Therefore strengthen the hands which hang down, and the feeble knees, and make straight paths for your feet, so that what is lame may not be dislocated, but rather be healed. Pursue peace with all people, and holiness, without which no one will see the Lord: looking carefully lest anyone fall short of the grace of God; lest any root of bitterness springing up cause trouble, and by this many become defiled...**
>
> **Hebrews 12:11-15**

I know these things hurt our ears. We want to hear scriptures that describe our expanded territories and rewards. We want to rejoice. But friends, take a moment and repent. Bitterness makes a person unclean. Trying to cover up our own sins corrupts those around us. Let the Spirit of Truth show you where you need to change so you can really heal. Take a better path where you won't fall down so often. Follow Christ, listen to Him, and when He stops to correct you, learn from Him. He's not trying to re-locate you to Easy Street. He wants to heal you where you live now. He sees the problem and calls it out into the open when He speaks to a demon in you. He wants to help you clean up, and bring you into the Father's house.

The spiritual side of staying "clean"

Emotional troubles cause physical problems. The spirit side of our wellbeing needs discipline. If a small sin takes root in your heart, you'll get one test after another so you can correct this problem that comes between you and God. He'll send that spirit away and expect you to learn to do the same on your own. He'll teach and counsel and show you how to do it, and when you pass the test, He'll walk with you. You're defiled if you refuse to clean up, but the Spirit of Christ makes it possible. There's your hope.

Think about the hope of change. Prepare for upheaval in the days ahead by practicing your job as a servant of the Most High God. Submit to punishment and correction if necessary. Time is short. If you live in peace, be in a state of readiness and service to those God puts in your path. If you live in turmoil, open your heart to His peace for stability.

All the while, let's prepare for the events that transpire in the spiritual world. When God's vengeance destroys wickedness, we'll see an end to the battle between good and evil. But for now, the times are evil. We need to learn what He hates and find out how He expects us to respond to it.

Sing to Him a new song; play skillfully with a shout of joy. For the word of the Lord is right, and all His work is done in truth. He loves righteousness and justice; the earth is full of the goodness of the Lord.

Psalm 33:3-5

Look around you to see the goodness of the Lord everywhere. Prepare to serve with a song in your heart. See your neighbors through eyes of love. Feed the hungry, clothe the naked, care for the orphans and widows as *His* love flows. Instruct children with truth and build them into good citizens and God-fearing adults. No sacrifice pleases Him like joyful obedience. Start today without lamenting about your past mistakes; shift into this kind of obedience with confidence.

God's kind of proactive love runs contrary to our nature. We sometimes settle into a passive, easy, feel-good faith, mistaking it for joyful worship.

Make sure selfishness is not holding you back. He's telling you to make a move, ready to obey...

... Draw near to God and He will draw near to you. Cleanse your hands, you sinners; and purify your hearts, you double-minded.
James 4:8

God recognizes our effort when we clean up and kneel before Him. We cannot show His great love to others without submitting to this regularly. By grace He saved us and forgave us, but we find it hard to extend the same kind of grace to others. In fact, we see other people's errors much more clearly than we see our own. Try to see by way of the spirit, through eyes of love and mercy.

Franklin Graham's love for Christ moved him to help people in the worst circumstances. He heads up Samaritan's Purse, bringing food and practical assistance to disaster areas, starving masses, people who hunger for hope. Always mindful of the spiritual side of the problem, he offers the good news of Christ Jesus, the love that motivates him. Recently he emailed an update on his missions, and his words described an urgent hopefulness: "The spiritual darkness and turmoil that is fast enveloping the world is only serving to prepare hearts to hear and receive the Gospel."

Recognize God's voice and live with a sense of peace during your own tribulations. The hope of change inspires us to endure and overcome. Hope does not disappoint.

Therefore, having been justified by faith, we have peace with God through our Lord Jesus Christ, through whom also we have access by faith into this grace in which we stand, and rejoice in hope of the glory of God. And not only *that,* but we also glory in tribulations, knowing that tribulation produces perseverance; and perseverance, character; and character, hope. Now hope does not disappoint, because the love of God has been poured out in our hearts by the Holy Spirit who was given to us.
Romans 5:1-5

LIVING BREAD

Let's go into the crowd and observe the people who followed Jesus across the Sea of Galilee and up the mountain to hear Him teach. They had been arriving in groups from all over the countryside to celebrate Passover together when they heard about this wise prophet. Stories began to circulate about His healing touch, and the joyous reports of miracles drew a crowd of Hebrew families. He rowed out into the lake with the disciples, and the crowds loaded up in boats to follow. On the other side, He hiked up the hillside, teaching them along the way.

Although He seemed to contradict the strict rules of the Pharisees, He spoke with authority about the laws of God. This strange man seemed to break some of the traditions, healing all sorts of afflictions, probably not washing up between touching the "unclean" and "untouchables" that came for help. By the end of the day, people were hungry. It was a long way down the mountain and across the lake on empty stomachs. The disciples looked around to see if anyone had enough food to share. They came up with five small loaves and two fish. Jesus calmly told the disciples:

Make the people sit down.

John 6:10a

Sit down. Expect God to provide for your every need, instead of worrying. If we hunger for something more in life, Jesus tells us to be still. Sit down and consider your Source.

And Jesus took the loaves, and when He had given thanks He distributed them to the disciples, and the disciples to those sitting down; and likewise of the fish, as much as they wanted.
John 6:11

They gave thanks for the small amount they had. More than five thousand men and their families waited to see what would happen next. I doubt that anyone who had listened and watched Him all day would have refused to sit down. Maybe they thought they'd each get a symbolic crumb. They'd have been willing to fast and pray all night with Him! So they sat down and gave thanks. That day they realized that *everything* starts with God and flows through Him. They had followed Jesus up the mountain and He taught them to count their blessings, however small, and watch them multiply. When all the people were well-fed, they gathered leftovers!

A wave of excitement grew in the crowd. They began to talk, "Is this the Messiah? Surely we've just eaten a meal with the King, himself!" Then, something odd happened.

Therefore when Jesus perceived that they were about to come and take Him by force to make Him king, He departed again to the mountain by Himself alone.
John 6:15

Jesus had no interest in being the kind of earthly king they expected. "My kingdom is not of this world," He would later explain. He refused to let them try to force an earthly crown on His head. His disciples went back down the mountain and shoved off in their boat to camp on the other side of the lake. Sometime after they left, Jesus literally walked across the dark waters to meet them in the boat.

Meanwhile, Jesus' impromptu demonstration of abundance filled the people's stomachs and they all stretched out under the stars to worship the One True God of plenty. Just like in the days of Moses when their forefathers witnessed miracles, they looked up in wonder and amazement together. I can hear the little groups, mothers whispering their children to sleep as the old men told tales of the mighty men of valor, and the youth gazed restlessly into the dark sky. Some had been healed of diseases and breathed pain-free sighs of relief. Demons had fled. Everyone, *everyone* was full. The Messiah had come.

The next morning they woke up hungry again, and He was not among them. After they crossed the lake in their boats, they ran to find Him, "When did you get here?"

Jesus answered them and said, "Most assuredly, I say to you, you seek Me, not because you saw the signs, but because you ate of the loaves and were filled. Do not labor for the food which perishes, but for the food which endures to everlasting life, which the Son of Man will give you, because God the Father has set His seal on Him."

John 6:26-27

Jesus wanted them to reflect on the spiritual nature of the events of the previous day. He asked them to consider how they spent their time, their goals and the things they worked toward. He pointed to their priorities and tried to get them to think of their eternal life in the kingdom of God.

They believed in Him and hoped to learn His ways. True seekers, they asked the right question:

What shall we do, that we may work the works of God?

John 6:28

To which Jesus declared:

This is the work of God, that you believe in Him whom He sent.

John 6:29b

Believing sometimes sounds just too easy. We want proof before we fall for something as simple as faith. So they asked Him:

> **What sign will You perform then, that we may see it and believe You? What work will You do? Our fathers ate the manna in the desert; as it is written, *'He gave them bread from heaven to eat.'***
>
> **John 6:30-31**

Notice their audacity! They actually ate the meal of the loaves and fishes just the day before, and then asked Him for another sign. They really believed *in* Him, but they wanted their Messiah to fulfill their expectations. Maybe they assumed that He'd gladly give them another meal. And just like Jesus always does, He turned it into a lesson.

> **I am the living bread which came down from heaven. If anyone eats of this bread, he will live forever; and the bread that I shall give is My flesh, which I shall give for the life of the world.**
>
> **John 6:51**

Scripture says that many believers turned away after that, not understanding how a man could give them His flesh to eat.

> **Therefore many of His disciples, when they heard *this,* said, "This is a hard saying; who can understand it?" When Jesus knew in Himself that His disciples complained about this, He said to them, "Does this offend you?"**
>
> **John 6:60-61**

Can't you just hear this conversation? It brings a smile to my face every time I read it! Jesus prepares us for power in the kingdom with hard teachings and repellent doctrines. He created us with a need to satisfy our **spiritual hunger**. It can only be filled with the mystery of His spiritual food. And we disciples continue to say, "Careful Jesus. We don't want to offend anyone!"

**Then Jesus said to the twelve, "Do you also want to go away?"
But Simon Peter answered Him, "Lord, to whom shall we go?
You have the words of eternal life. Also we have come to believe
and know that You are the Christ, the Son of the living God."**

John 6:67-69

Jesus sacrificed His body on earth in order to fill us with His eternal substance. Until now, your past experiences may have established what your religious life looks like. I hope you still hunger for more. As you begin to wash your hands in preparation for a spiritual feast in the Rest, remember that God expects you to show up at the table for every family meal in the kingdom of heaven.

Now listen carefully to Jesus' response one day when the Pharisees asked why the disciples did not always wash their hands before eating bread, a practice which was a tradition of their elders.

**Hypocrites! Well did Isaiah prophesy about you, saying: 'These
people draw near to Me with their mouth, and honor Me with
their lips, but their heart is far from Me. And in vain they
worship Me, teaching as doctrines the commandments of men.'**

Matthew 15:7-9

Jesus cautioned them about using their religious customs to validate their spiritual condition. He warned about fanaticism and pointed out that they did not keep the true spirit of the law. The disciples worried that He might insult some of these men. They respected the leaders in their synagogue. Reading the context carefully, you see that they spoke about hand washing. The rabbis passed down complex rules about clean and unclean as they tried to work out how to obey God's Laws. Jewish people never ate a meal without washing up first, and now this motley crew had been seen eating grain right off the stalk. Jesus' statements did not change God's commandments regarding forbidden foods in the Old Testament.[61]

---

61   Matthew 15:17-18

When He had called the multitude to *Himself*, He said to them, "Hear and understand: Not what goes into the mouth defiles a man; but what comes out of the mouth, this defiles a man."
Matthew 15:10-11

He spoke of matters of the heart (spiritual), not the stomach (physical). He wants us to acquire a bitter taste for those unclean thoughts passing through our lips. He wants us to purify our minds as we filter our own thoughts with His wisdom.

So Jesus said, "Are you also still without understanding? Do you not yet understand that whatever enters the mouth goes into the stomach and is eliminated? But those things which proceed out of the mouth come from the heart, and they defile a man. For out of the heart proceed evil thoughts, murders, adulteries, fornications, thefts, false witness, blasphemies. These are *the things* which defile a man, but to eat with unwashed hands does not defile a man."
Matthew 15:16-20

We try to be spiritual but our bodies get in the way. Religion seems to get in the way, too, and instead of watching every word we speak, we debate about doctrines and traditions. But when you listen to Jesus, He makes it very personal. Our craving for the reassurance of tradition keeps us from traversing the conflicting area between our comfort zone and the Way. Human nature tells us to savor little morsels of our old way of life. Sometimes we busy ourselves with the commandments of men, while we completely miss out on the Rest.

Some think that the word of God, easily misinterpreted, should not offend anyone. Believers consume fast-food sermons and never sit down to fill themselves with mature teachings in Bible study. Work, entertainment and comfort become their centers of attention. Participating in church activities as a means to spiritual fulfillment, people mistakenly try to celebrate God's goodness without obedience. They begin to think of ways to achieve perfection and peace on their own terms, making their activities about Him, yet without Him. God refuses to compromise about the personal growth that leads to sanctification.

Blessed *are* those who hunger and thirst for righteousness, for they shall be filled.

Matthew 5:6

As Christians, we may not know that we starve for the word of God. We have heard it often and studied it now and then, but have not allowed the words to pierce us to the point that they divide soul from spirit, judging the attitudes of our hearts. *Ouch! We think it will be too painful to bear or too mysterious to believe in.* It will be the end of us in all our glory- or misery-or whatever state we are in. And oh, how we worship the status quo in our world today. We do not even want to admit that we need to change.

If you follow Jesus, you do not have to appear to be perfect. Your actions of love reveal His Spirit to others, and He takes care of all the details. Jesus calls us into His word to find contentment that defies rational explanation.

...for I have learned in whatever state I am, to be content: I know how to be abased, and I know how to abound. Everywhere and in all things I have learned both to be full and to be hungry, both to abound and to suffer need. I can do all things through Christ who strengthens me.

Philippians 4:11b-13

Allow God to bring you closer to the realization of a rich spirit-filled life, regardless of your physical circumstances. He knows your imperfections, but He loves that about you! Fill up with the truth of scripture. Simply tap into your source of endless love, Love Himself.

REACHING FOR HEAVEN

At the last supper, Jesus told the disciples that He would be leaving soon. Looking closely at His words, we see that He promised the ability to "see" Him in the spirit so that **"anyone who has faith in Me will do what I have been doing."** [62] One of the disciples posed the question,

> **Lord, how is it that You will manifest Yourself to us, and not to the world?**
>
> **John 14:22b**

"Keep My word." Jesus explained gently. **"Then My Father will love you and make our home with you**." They wondered *how* to stay in contact after He left them behind. He gave them clues to the spirit realm. We strain to hear the answer, too. Instead of sending us on some complicated spiritual quest to see God, Jesus continues to open the screen door of our heart and call us in for supper. If we love Him, we're part of His family and He will come and make a home with us. Yes, His Father, *our Father*, will be there too.

As long as we think of God in far-off heavenly places, our faith,

---

62   John 14:12

stretched to the limit of our sound reasoning, floats away from us in a puff with the slightest distraction. We need more than just talk about Him. We need more than stories. When we find ourselves praying as if He's out there somewhere, but not here with us, we tend to sign off with a "good-bye for now" mind-set, and then try to live purely in the physical realm until we call Him again.

Jesus explained that He and the Father would come to us because we love Him, indicating that there would be no distance between us. "When and where should we meet with You?" That's our question. We really want to know. "Here and now, without regard to time or space. In other words, any time, anywhere, you'll be able to see me," He seems to tell us. Sometimes I wonder if our technology hints at just such a revelation, similar to talking on a cell phone or having a live conversation on the computer. We keep asking, "How do we connect?" **"Keep My commands."** Jesus gave the disciples such a simple answer, but we want to clarify it.

God created us in His image and assigns responsibilities to each one in His household. He spans our perception of distance to live with us. "All commands?" We need to know if He made allowances for our disobedience. "If you love Me, you will keep my commands." [63]

I doubt that the disciples really understood the implication of celebrating the commanded Holy Days of Passover with the *Passover Sacrifice Himself*. They understood that the entire Torah represented the commands of God for the Israelites. Their lives, already filled with command-keeping traditions, required no adjustments to meet those requirements, yet they naturally felt puzzled about this new revelation.

We continue to ask questions of our Lord. "Were you talking about the Ten Commandments?"

We want Jesus to clarify this for the non-Jewish branches He grafted into the vine. I see the smile on His radiant face as He gives me the typical Rabbinic-style answer that spurs me to dig deeper into His word. "Yes and no. There's so much more. If you want Me to live with you, you need to enlarge your thinking to include all of Me and all of the kingdom; then you can follow Me."

---

63   John 14:23

Pressing to understand how, when and where from our perspective, we remember that God connected us to the physical world temporarily. While we live here, Jesus brings us into the kingdom of heaven, establishing an intimate association and a fruitful life. He painted a picture of the kind of increase that He expected from His followers. He described how a spiritual man can bear fruit while He lives on earth.

I am the vine, you *are* the branches. He who abides in Me, and I in him, bears much fruit; for without Me you can do nothing. If anyone does not abide in Me, he is cast out as a branch and is withered; and they gather them and throw *them* into the fire, and they are burned. If you abide in Me, and My words abide in you, you will ask what you desire, and it shall be done for you. By this My Father is glorified, that you bear much fruit; so you will be My disciples.

John 15:5-8

This passage assures us of the absolute certainty of our source. I take great comfort in knowing that God allows us to meander toward heaven as long as our spiritual intent is rooted in faith in Him. Drawn to His light, we grow. But any gardener knows that if a branch shoots off in the wrong direction, it must be pruned and discarded for the plant to produce well. God created us to grow closer to Him by obeying His commands as we live on the vine.

Some people think of contact with God as a sort of crisis hot-line, in case of an emergency. As we mature in faith, our prayers include many facets of confession, petition, gratitude and worship. Eventually, God hopes we ask questions, listen to His reply, reason out the answers in His word, and then come back to Him excited about our new revelation! That connection, becoming a part of His household and following the Master Teacher, Jesus Himself, hints at our eternal destiny. What joy we give to our Father when we connect with Him in such a way while we live on earth! The angels, purely spiritual beings, wonder why He loves us so. I wonder, too, because most of us rarely think about giving our Father joy.

We usually want Him to give us something.

Sometimes when we call upon God in prayer and the outcome appears vague, we wonder why it didn't work. Look closer at our ideas about reaching for our heavenly Father in this way. Congregations recite memorized prayers. Families pray together before a meal. Alone, in silence we share our needs, joys and sorrows with our heavenly Father.

And when you pray, do not use vain repetitions as the heathen do. For they think that they will be heard for their many words. Therefore, do not be like them. For your Father knows the things you have need of before you ask Him.

Matthew 6:7-8

If you reason, "God already knows what we need, so why pray?" then you miss the point. He wants to have a real conversation with you, hear you out, consider your intentions and give you His thoughts on the situation. Your faith that the *Creator controls the entire creation* allows you to pray with confidence of the outcome. Your words come alive with power, not when you repeat them, but when you firmly believe in the force of His Spirit behind them. Your action and/or apathy reveal the aim of your heart, regardless of your expressions of prayer. Further, God does not hear sinners:

Now we know that God does not hear sinners; but if anyone is a worshiper of God and does His will, He hears him.

John 9:31

I've learned that this quotation surprises most Christians and sends them rushing to their Bibles to check for truth. Nothing makes me happier! Our preconceived notions about God sometimes represent our childhood lessons, the baby food of believers. Begin letting the totality of scripture nourish your spiritual garden for extra fruit. Because we all sin, most people ignore that statement about God not hearing the prayers of sinners. This serious matter deserves our attention. He expects us to seek Him with a commitment to grow.

At every level of maturity, the Spirit reveals a new awareness of sin far beyond what we understood before that. Simultaneously, He opens our eyes to a more intimate fellowship with the Father Himself as we learn His ways.

Thank goodness the scriptures confirm that God hears the prayers of *repentant sinners*. I imagine joyous shouts going up from the host of heaven when we call out to Him with a contrite spirit that's willing to change directions. If you feel down and out, listen to this:

He shall regard the prayer of the destitute, and shall not despise their prayer.

Psalm 102:17

John the Baptist called people to personally and publicly repent as preparation for **"all flesh to see the salvation of God"**.[64] He told the Pharisees they didn't have a prayer when they came out to see what was going on with the crowd by the river:

Then Jerusalem, all Judea, and all the region around the Jordan went out to him and were baptized by him in the Jordan, confessing their sins. But when he saw many of the Pharisees and Sadducees coming to his baptism, he said to them, "Brood of vipers! Who warned you to flee from the wrath to come? Therefore bear fruits worthy of repentance."

Matthew 3:5-8

These men thought about God all the time. They memorized His word and taught it. Yet God quit listening to them when pride and selfish ambition hardened their hearts. A person who refuses to turn away from his own sin spouts empty prayers with no power to produce righteous fruit. If the words themselves stimulate a response in the kingdom, it comes in the form of another opportunity to repent.

---

64   Luke 3:3-6

If we say that we have no sin, we deceive ourselves, and the truth is not in us. If we confess our sins, He is faithful and just to forgive us *our* sins and to cleanse us from all unrighteousness. If we say that we have not sinned, we make Him a liar, and His word is not in us.

1 John 1:8-10

Imperfections and all, we want to stay on the vine and avoid the necessary pruning. John wrote to the early Christians urging them to let the Holy Spirit change their life so they could *really abide* with God. He told them to detect lies and deceiving spirits based on a simple test:

Who is a liar but he who denies that Jesus is the Christ? He is antichrist who denies the Father and the Son. Whoever denies the Son does not have the Father either; he who acknowledges the Son has the Father also.

1 John 2:22-23

Pause here to note the clear description of antichrist. Anyone who denies Jesus as the anointed Son of God carries the spirit of the antichrist. You need to be aware of this and reject their teachings if they offer spiritual guidance. If you know someone who expresses such beliefs, a spirit of antichrist might be present. You cannot reason with that person and expect the spirit to go away peacefully, but when they've had enough of the hollow ideology, they can ask Christ Himself to send it running with His glance. The spirit of the antichrist has been causing doubt and confusion for at least 2000 years that we know of, and occupies many mainstream religions today.

Now let's get back to the point: living with God. As members of God's family, we recognize our own faults and make a conscious effort not to repeat them. We ask Christ to show us how to get rid of them again and again sometimes, but just like little children, our attention spans are short.

My little children, these things I write to you, so that you may not sin. And if anyone sins, we have an Advocate with the Father, Jesus Christ the righteous. And He Himself is the propitiation for our sins, and not for ours only but also for the whole world.

1 John 2:1-2

The whole world benefits from Christ's ongoing advocacy. He's actively involved in our defense. He teaches us to discern the spirits that war against our Father's house within us and learn to cut them off decisively as we mature. He wants to help us improve our ability to overcome the flesh. If we avoid spiritual growth, then ungodly character traits grow instead.

He who says, "I know Him," and does not keep His commandments, is a liar, and the truth is not in him. But whoever keeps His word, truly the love of God is perfected in him. By this we know that we are in Him.

1 John 2:4-5

I'm not perfect, but I want the love of God to be perfected in me, so I resolve to know Him and keep His word. No one is faultless, but children of God refuse the practice of *deliberate* sin and submit to the sanctification process. I cannot overstate the importance of our attitude toward God. When a believer sins willfully, knowing that their Father offers forgiveness, they invite deceiving spirits into their heart. This double minded decision sets them up for earthly calamity and the kind of childish fear that lingers many long years at the veil, waiting for the promises of heaven. Some people want to know just how much leeway God will actually give them in their worldly cycle. We don't need to ask, "How much does God love me?" but "How much do I love God?" Do we love Him enough to do discern both good and evil?

But solid food belongs to those who are of full age, that is, those who by reason of use have their senses exercised to discern both good and evil.

Hebrews 5:14

When we make an effort to recognize the difference between good and evil in our own heart, and consistently choose the good, we mature into fruit-bearing branches. However, a stubborn refusal to repent reduces our life works to withered branches piled up to be discarded. We must get past the elementary principles of faith if we expect to enjoy the fruits of living on the vine.

Therefore, leaving the discussion of the elementary *principles* of Christ, let us go on to perfection, not laying again the foundation of repentance from dead works...

Hebrews 6:1a

Repentance. Genuine repentance. It bears repeating because we just get so entwined in our excuses. If recurring feelings of regret linger within us because our works are "dead," get out the pruning shears. We need to examine ourselves instead of blaming others, until we uncover a habitual sin that won't let go. Spirits of gossip, slander, lust, resentment, grudges, addictions, self-absorption and fearfulness tend to live just below the surface of the flesh. God calls His righteous offspring to get rid of these pests which hinder spiritual growth and dissipate the will to obey Him. **By reason of use we exercise our senses to discern good and evil.**

Everyone knows that gardeners who yield the best produce maintain their fields constantly, removing pests, pruning, fertilizing, digging up weeds, and even letting the land rest. Our daily prayer time should include these exercises.

Our Father hears His children. He walked with righteous men in Old Testament times. Now, with the Holy Spirit, we truly unite with our Father through Christ. He connects us with the kingdom while we're earthbound. Every thought sends a signal out into His spiritual kingdom. Jesus tried to explain it, but we just couldn't make sense of what He said. Any attempt to limit our God to the physical world sets us up for disappointment. Our faith grows in our thoughts, our imagination, and extends beyond our words into the lives of those who hear them. Members of God's household grow to learn the love language of mercy, truth and justice.

Therefore, laying aside all malice, all deceit, hypocrisy, envy, and all evil speaking, as newborn babes, desire the pure milk of the word, that you may grow thereby, if indeed you have tasted that the Lord is gracious. Coming to Him as to a living stone, rejected indeed by men, but chosen by God and precious, you also, as living stones, are being built up a spiritual house, a holy priesthood, to offer up spiritual sacrifices acceptable to God through Jesus Christ.

1 Peter 2:1-5

I've watched a master stonemason work. He looks over the pile and picks up the rock he wants. He chips and breaks off the edges, and when he lays it up with mortar atop the other stones, he rarely takes it off again. He takes a pile of rough hewn rocks and builds a beautiful place to live. In the same way, we are a part of something greater than our individual selves.

Living on the vine means we care about the rich heritage of the patriarchs, and claim their stories as our own. We live, grafted into the family of Abraham. When we produce fruit, we go to work distributing the love of our Father, carrying all the authority of His sons and daughters representing Him on earth. As children of God mature, we turn away from selfish desires to seek the will of our Father.

I press toward the goal for the prize of the upward call of God in Christ Jesus. Therefore let us, as many as are mature, have this mind; and if in anything you think otherwise, God will reveal even this to you. Nevertheless, to *the degree* that we have already attained, let us walk by the same rule, let us be of the same mind.

Philippians 3:14-16

The Spirit of God turns our mind away from the flesh so we bring respect and honor to the family. Jesus enables us to represent Him in the kingdom with increasing ability. We begin to participate in kingdom business, no longer focused on physical concerns. Far beyond our childish prayers, we never ask for something that would harm the vine. When we make a mistake with pure motives, the love of Christ perfects, corrects, and at the same time protects us.

Regardless of the sinful cycle each man chooses for a time, the Holy Spirit offers the power to change directions. It represents an act of humility when we ask the Spirit to modify our behavior. When we love and study God's word, He sends control far greater than our fleshy resolve. He raises us from our deadly pattern of thinking to our pre-ordained place as His offspring. With once small glimpse of this reality, no earthly detail affects us the same way again.

Think of yourself, a believer, as a tender vine growing closer to heaven every moment. When you make a mistake and call upon God, an earnest prayer of repentance bends your branch back in the right direction. You unintentionally veered off toward some worldly destination, and now turn toward Him again. Your heart remains tender enough to keep you steadily growing toward heaven. If, however, you get up from that prayer behaving no differently than before, God may allow you to go through a pruning as He cuts away the hardened wayward branches of disobedience and puts them in the fire. Expect discipline and more lessons.

Praise God for His patience! As we grow toward Him, He penetrates us with the warmth of forgiveness. As long as we remain tender vines, we see our errors and learn from them, correcting the direction of our thoughts. If our words and actions do not represent Him, then we can plan for a disappointing harvest. If our branches tend toward worldly destinations for our own purposes, we must undergo a severe pruning again.

I wonder if some believers have been pruned to the point that they have nothing left of themselves but a large stub. They have lived on the vine a long time, but continue behavior that must be cut away again and again. A severely pruned plant looks dead for a while, but then the green shoots come forth in the spring with another chance to grow in the right direction.

How do we produce the righteous fruit that scripture speaks of?

I beseech you therefore, brethren, by the mercies of God, that you present your bodies a living sacrifice, holy, acceptable to God, *which is* your reasonable service. And do not be conformed to this world, but be transformed by the renewing of your mind, that you may prove what *is* that good and acceptable and perfect will of God.

Romans 12:1-2

Open your mind to God's instruction and receive a surge of eternal energy. We make thousands of choices every day, forming our remarkable spiral toward heaven. God allows His nature to flow through our branches and out through our fingertips and lips as we grow toward His light. Our words reflect God's forgiveness, the love language that builds God's kingdom and feeds His people with encouragement and joy.

We give Him our troubles and replace them with our obedience. We ask. God responds.

Now this is the confidence that we have in Him, that if we ask anything according to His will, He hears us. And if we know that He hears us, whatever we ask, we know that we have the petitions that we have asked of Him.

1 John 5:14-15

Jesus calls us heavenward in our confidence of these truths. I know that spiritual growth does not just happen. We reach for it, stretch out and seek it. Rooted securely in His salvation, sprinkled with grace, we grow toward His light.

GROWING UP IN OUR PRAYERS

I want extraordinary things to happen when I pray, just as Jesus promised. With childlike inquisitiveness, I continued to ask God what He wants us to understand about prayer. Jesus led me to the garden to see a tiny mustard seed again. He patiently explained that, just as a child grows, faith grows too. He reminded me that God gives faith as a gift, a small seed planted in our spirit. It may lie dormant, neglected perhaps, yet when the mustard seed sprouts and gets proper cultivation, it grows into the largest of all the garden plants. When we make choices to nurture our faith, a harvest of good quality grows up and reveals the power of God.

"Pray just like you're talking to Me now," I heard Jesus chuckle as He placed another seed in the garden and patted the dirt carefully. "Your prayers are like this little spade I'm using. Together we use them to get at the root of important issues in life. As you mature, your prayers develop into power-tools because you've spent so much time with me learning in the kingdom... You'll start thinking like me because you imitate me."

... but also if you say to this mountain, "Be removed and cast into the sea," it will be done. And whatever things you ask in prayer, believing, you will receive.

Matthew 21:21b-22

158

His bold statement continues to stretch my imagination. I believe He planted great potential within us and nurtures us until we discover it. However, before we think about maturing in our prayer life, we need to clarify and add a word of caution here. Many false teachers present this "asking in prayer" principle as a formula, and people itch to hear the prosperity doctrines that focus on such earthly outcomes. Nothing could be further from the truth. Beware of name-it-and-claim-it religions where Satan uses scripture to lure spiritual seekers back into the flesh. Our mental capacity to focus our own convictions *may* trigger a tangible result, but God's law prohibits using knowledge of spiritual power for worldly gain. There is a fine line between witchcraft and the kind of power that Christ spoke about. The difference lies in *whom we serve*. Praying for possessions and success in this world, we make them master and lord in our lives. They will possess us when we receive them. If you tried such a method, and it didn't work, praise God! If you're surrounded with abundance in your life, ask God where He wants you to use it, and focus on the family business.

Jesus invites us to explore the mystery of prayer power to see our wholehearted faith working in practical ways. It's mandatory for sons and daughters of the kingdom to practice God's laws and use their words wisely before He gives such spiritual authority. We cannot teach another until we know it for ourselves, and we cannot learn it until we remove all selfish motives. Then He shows us, one by one, the truth of His spiritual supremacy in our lives. Our heartfelt desire to draw people to God's kingdom intensifies as we grow in this knowledge.

Get a fresh outlook on your own God-given spiritual qualities. In the following passage, visualize yourself responding to the words as if they were written to you. I put my personal response in parentheses.

The LORD is gracious and full of compassion, slow to anger and great in mercy. *(These are family traits! God's grace makes up our character, too.)* **The LORD is good to all,** *(Everyone?)* **and His tender mercies are over all His works.** *(I'm one of His works, aren't you?)* **All your works** *(All creation everywhere.)* **shall praise You, O LORD, and Your saints** *(They are everywhere, too.)* **shall**

159

bless You. *(Did you know that God likes to be blessed, too?)* **They shall speak of the glory of Your kingdom,** *(Notice what He wants to hear in our conversations.)* **and talk of Your power,** *(He's in control.)* **to make known to the sons of men His mighty acts,** *(God wants everyone to recognize His activity all around us.)* **and the glorious majesty of His kingdom.** *(Celebrate the victory of living with power and authority in the heavenly realm.)*

Psalm 145:8-12

With a desire to be like Him, we're more likely to show mercy to people even though they cause problems for us and appear to be shackled with sin. We praise God for the glory of His power. He wants to reveal Himself to others, and we join Him in that purpose. That's why we pray and enter into a private place in the kingdom where we can clearly hear God. Regardless of our spiritual maturity, if we serve Christ, we cannot make a mistake in persistent prayer. Whether God's objective is our aim or we miss the mark with our limited understanding, the kingdom operates with one huge overarching purpose that embraces all people: LOVE.

Suppose we prayed for a loved one who struggles with sin, and their problems get worse. Maybe we just said, "God, please help them." We watched, yet our prayers *seemed* to go unanswered as we hoped their *situation* would improve. Look into the kingdom to find out what really happened. Maybe a spirit of jealousy, anger or fear troubles them. Seeing the real problem, we realize they've been fighting a serious battle and losing. They ran away from God's blessings to pursue their own ideas (yes, we've all done that), but they stopped and cried out to Him in frustration when the situation worsened. There's the answer to our prayer! We asked God to draw them close to Him and He heard us. Now He's positioned for **mighty acts**. Maybe they will listen to the **saints speak of the glory of His kingdom**. If not, He still loves them with such passion! They represent one of His most **beloved works** and His **tender mercies** are all over them. That's all we need to know. God's in charge. Instead of worrying about their sinfulness, we see a window of opportunity to encourage them and plant seeds of faith. When our intent lines up with God's plan to build the

160

kingdom, He gives us a chance to join Him in the effort.

Should we point out their errors, and tell them about God's condemnation? It's not helpful to warn someone about the pit if they've already fallen into it. We need to show them the way out, the rescue that Jesus offers. Tell them the truth about forgiveness instead.

If someone rejected your attempt at "Christian outreach" in the past, perhaps they felt a spirit of arrogance from you. Love them. God will give you another chance as you both grow a little more. I can't find a place in the Bible that instructs me to decide whether God plans to condemn another person for eternity, so I am always taken aback when Christians talk and worry about someone going to hell. We might serve Him better by rooting out the sins in our own life, one by one, and offering mercy to those who find His love elusive in this dark world. When our light shines into their darkness with hope that only God offers, they see love, not condemnation. Christ wants everyone, *everyone* to come to Him. I'm convinced He'll do everything He can to bring in each lost sheep.

Our job involves following the Creator Himself and pointing out His greatness so others will join Him too. Pray for someone entangled in sin with His compassion and kindness, knowing that God has a plan for their life, despite all appearances. Believers need to be sure there's love, not condemnation, in their heart for the recipient before they speak. Love covers a multitude of sins and God's laws are sufficient for pointing them out.

If you feel superior to someone when you're sharing God's word, stop and look for a sneaky demon lurking in your kingdom near the temple. Speaking the word of God with a selfish motive or pride is Satan's all-time favorite technique. If he can get a believer to do this, his deception wreaks havoc in that family or community of faith.

Jesus always ignites the hearts of His brethren with love. When we pray for someone to draw closer to God, and they're not ready, God may allow the adversary to turn up the heat for repentance, purification, refinement and growth. When we pray for their smooth landing, we inadvertently ask God to remove an opportunity for their faith to grow. Adversity leads us to rely on Him more, not less. Such discipline may not *feel* like love, but we need to remember that our Lord grieves when His children suffer from disobedience.

In all circumstances, when someone stops, admits their error and turns toward Jesus Christ, He responds. God hears *that prayer* loud and clear.

Sometimes we confuse repentance (admitting our sins and stopping them) with talking about our problems and saying we're sorry. We try to incorporate this into our prayer life instead of using the knowledge of God to purify ourselves of error. God's word puts us right in the middle of poignant lessons of adjustments and radical changes that do not fit into our plans. We cannot pray for our plans and expect blessings while ignoring what He tells us to do. We must be willing to let His Spirit drastically change our lives to accomplish His purpose.

We continue to pray, recognizing that God can accomplish all things with us or without us. He is working all the time, but not necessarily on our schedule. Spiritually born-again, believers follow their destiny as eternal beings, participating in the full force of His power when we mature. He is not in a hurry like we are. We need to understand His ways so that we recognize His authority and control.

> **The LORD upholds all who fall, and raises up all who are bowed down. ...You open Your hand and satisfy the desire of every living thing. The LORD is righteous in all His ways, gracious in all His works. The LORD is near to all who call upon Him, to all who call upon Him in truth.**
>
> **Psalm 145:14-18**

Jesus is truth. Truth sends you back into the world with a powerful humility. We must never think that we know enough to make it on our own. Jesus delights in teaching the mysteries of the kingdom to those who approach it with childlike innocence.

> **In that hour Jesus rejoiced in the Spirit and said, "I thank You, Father, Lord of heaven and earth, that You have hidden these things from *the* wise and prudent and revealed them to babes. Even so, Father, for so it seemed good in Your sight.**
>
> **Luke 10:21**

Naturally, at first we tend to focus our prayers on needs of the physical world, not God's kingdom. That's infantile thinking for eternal creatures. Christ sees our immature spiritual development and loves to watch us grow. He's not interested in our capacity to participate in great miracles. To the extent that we resist *spiritual* growth and cling to dead works (worldly results), we disobey God.

BABY STEPS INTO THE KINGDOM

We live in a time when the virtues of discipline and patience seem less important than our immediate desires. This need for instant gratification pervades our culture and weakens a believer in their prayer life. We sometimes fail to reflect the power and authority of a son of God, but more closely resemble a child asking for candy at dinnertime. The child thinks only of what he wants, but the good parent would never consider giving in to their desire. As the child gets older, however, he's allowed to experiment with free will, entering a season of growth by trial, error, discipline and practice. In the same way, God allows us to make the wrong choices as part of our growth.

Jesus suggested we move mountains by faith in God, rather than achieve God-sized results on our own, pointing out a huge realm of possibilities when it comes to our eternal destiny. We shall tell the mountains to move when they stand in the way of God's purpose, and reveal the majesty of our Father for all to see.

God wants an invigorating discussion with sons and daughters who take on some level of authority in the family business. Does He hope we'll mature enough to sit down and share joyful news of kingdom-building and listen to His plans? Is He drawing us out of our childish prayers to claim righteous influence in the spiritual world? Let's repent of our idle unbelief and demonstrate the truth. Christ commended those who witnessed miracles of faith because they saw into the kingdom.

> **Then He turned to *His* disciples and said privately, "Blessed *are* the eyes which see the things you see..."**
>
> **Luke 10:23a**

My stepfather made a little wooden plaque which sums it: "A wise man knows how little he knows." When we start thinking that we know enough about faith to commence with the mountain-moving, God may detect a lack of humility. This sets us up for another one of His tests. Notice the fine line between rejoicing when you participate in a miracle and claiming the power for your flesh. You can say, "Halleluiah! Give God the glory!" But He knows if your words ring true. To work in the Father's business, we must give up our own agenda and surrender personal desires.

You enter the kingdom as His child and the Holy Spirit teaches. When your thoughts line up with His, your prayers reflect God's spiritual intent, not your physical needs. Does this mean that you cannot ask for things you need? Just ask Him. He wants you to come to Him to discuss your inner desires and secret longings. He wants to bless your house and heal your pain. He knows what you need and cares about you. He wants you to choose Him over everything and everyone, just as He chose you.

He moves mountains whenever He pleases, and invites the righteous to see in the spirit.[65] But His overarching rationale involves eternity, not our physical circumstances. Today, we move *spiritual* mountains out of the way.

The Holy Spirit came upon the new believers during the Holy Days of Pentecost, creating quite a commotion. Crowds witnessed the event, many people believed, and Peter explained:

> **This Jesus God has raised up, of which we are all witnesses. Therefore being exalted to the right hand of God, and having received from the Father the promise of the Holy Spirit, He poured out this which you now see and hear. For David did not ascend into the heavens, but he says himself: "The LORD said to my Lord, *Sit at My right hand, till I make Your enemies Your footstool.*"**
>
> **Acts 2:32-35**

---

65   2 Kings 2:9-12

From Jesus' vantage point at the right hand of the Father, the enemy cowers in defeat, trampled by the sons of the kingdom. Yet many believers seem discouraged and unaware of this arrangement.

Some well-intentioned believers may have accumulated partial truths about prayer, thinking the same thoughts and doing the same things over and over, asking God to fix what He will. Often we mimic prayers, going to Him with a list of other people who need healing, thanking Him for our blessings at dinner, and asking Him to provide for our loved ones. Then we say "Amen" and go our way unchanged in our encounter with Him. We pray on the surface, but God wants us to talk things out with Him thoughtfully. In fact, He knows that a real encounter with Him would change everything in our life. Nothing would be the same!

How often do believers try to fit God in a predictable box that we can control, thinking we can close the lid on Him after we pray and then go about our own business? Jesus told us to go beyond vain repetitions to an earnest prayer that connects us to our Creator. Just like any relationship, we tell how we feel, talk about our inner struggles, celebrate our victories together, and listen. Identifying our spiritual "enemies" and going to our Father to discuss the issues of life, we put forth the effort that goes into a vibrant faith of worship and obedience. When we relate to God with every word that comes out of our mouth, everything we choose to look at, and every step we take, we live in constant prayer.

When Christ taught us how to pray, He sandwiched the Lord's Prayer in between teachings on a wide range of topics.[66] Profound words poured out from the mind of God that urged the listeners to adjust their thinking and behavior.

For your Father knows the things you have need of before you ask Him.

Matthew 6:8b

With limited understanding of the power we embody, we find it difficult to arrange our lives around the knowledge of God, putting the kingdom

---

66   Matthew 5-6

first. Who works to keep it a closely held secret, if not the Adversary? It's his job to oppose us, and our job to push the devil out of the way and pursue this knowledge. We train to defend our kingdom within, keeping the words of our Father in the center of our heart where they will reign over our emotions and feelings. Listen for His words, wait to hear them, concentrate on them and apply them to your flesh. God's Word, Jesus Christ, gives you the power to overcome the evil (selfish) inclination and do the will of our Father.

> **But now you yourselves are to put off all these: anger, wrath, malice, blasphemy, filthy language out of your mouth. Do not lie to one another, since you have put off the old man with his deeds, renewed in knowledge according to the image of Him who created him.**
>
> **Colossians 3:8-9**

We project a genuine new image as children of God. The old man (self) and his deeds behind us, we would not consider wearing the filthy rags of our old sins again. Let me give you an example. If you quit smoking cigarettes, you sense the smell more acutely on others, as the nicotine soaks into people's clothing and seeps out of their pores. You no longer want to breathe it or be around it. You know that you don't want it anymore, because you want to stay healthy and feel good about overcoming the addiction. In the same way, other sins involving the mouth cling to us like filthy habits, too. We need to recognize such subtle addictions of the flesh and outsmart the devil. If we really want to reflect the image of our Creator, we must make the effort.

I want to be renewed in knowledge as the Holy Spirit teaches me how to pray and what to pray for! We don't ask for everything we once desired because we live as new beings looking for *things unseen* to the untrained eye. The strife and worry of life give way to the spectacle of activity in the spirit; we notice the miraculous "coincidences" that surround us each day.

Yes, mature believers possess power and assurance, although it may not be as tangible as the signs and wonders you've been watching for.[67] You may question why anyone would seek such invisible solace, until you, too, reel from the overwhelming evil that encroaches in your life. You've tried everything, and now it comes down to the truth:

...let us draw near with a true heart in full assurance of faith, having our hearts sprinkled from an evil conscience and our bodies washed with pure water.

Hebrews 10:22

If Jesus changes us into a suitable dwelling place for the Spirit of God, then you can be sure that this cleansing process makes us suitable for healthy earthly relationships. Obedience to the truth keeps us pure. God's word resides in our hearts and minds as a perpetual purification system. The Word, Jesus Himself, provides His Spirit to help us obey God's laws of love.

...Since you have purified your souls in obeying the truth through the Spirit in sincere love of the brethren, love one another fervently with a pure heart...

1 Peter 1:22

In song, reverence, and innocent love we pray. God laughs, cries, and rejoices with us. Sometimes He has to turn His face away from us in disgust. He already lives in our relationships. He is available 24/7. No problem too big. No sin too bad. He's seen it all. No situation too silly or severe.

...praying always with all prayer and supplication in the Spirit...

Ephesians 6:18a

We make the best decisions when we let God in on them. Remember, He knows the outcome.

---

67   Acts 1:4-8

Jesus could have healed all of His countrymen instantly, but instead, He touched the lives of those He personally encountered along the way. We need to understand this if we want our prayers to line up with His will. Healing, miracles or answered prayers, per se, do not establish a strong faith. It's the other way around. Faith in the unseen, a whisper of hope, a word spoken, righteous thinking, a servant's heart - these seem to be the catalysts that summon God's activity. Signs and wonders may affirm our faith and encourage us to grow, just as suffering and trials do. Yet our distress, our very need for the miracle in the first place, forces us to search for Him personally and ask Him to take notice of our situation. The question arises: If we never reached those low spots where we seek Him fervently, then would we simply ignore Him?

With a few rare exceptions, I suspect the answer is yes. For this reason, sons of God must use proper judgment when they pray. God's answer always leans toward the same result: repentance and reconciliation with Him.

When you pray, consider your place in the kingdom with Jesus. Think of the things that He suffered for you. Remember that His peers despised Him before you pray for your own recognition. Take heart in the fact that He, too, was rejected and misunderstood when you discuss your situation with Him. Understand that He was wounded for your transgressions that you might be healed in your spirit. Think about HIM and find strength. Ask for His wisdom as you form the words of your prayers.

Rejoice in the Lord always. Again I will say, rejoice! Let your gentleness be known to all men. The Lord *is* at hand. Be anxious for nothing, but in everything by prayer and supplication, with thanksgiving, let your requests be made known to God; and the peace of God, which surpasses all understanding, will guard your hearts and minds through Christ Jesus.

Philippians 4:4-7

We live in the fragrance of God's blessings all around us. Our answered prayers dance in the twinkle of a child's eyes. They show up in reconciled families gathered around a dying parent's bedside. Our answered prayers materialize in the form of hardships overcome, words carefully chosen, generosity poured out by His servants. God calls us to take a step forward into His Rest where He guards our hearts and minds.

God answers our prayers before we utter them. He fills us with a love overflowing that washes away the worst problems and spills out into life. We find purpose in our awareness of this love. Our eagerness to share it expands as we mature with our baby steps of faith. Baby steps of the children of God, growing into sons and daughters of the kingdom, marching in rhythm to the victorious power and presence of the Holy Spirit!

A Prayer for Us

God promises to reveal His righteous work to His children and allows us to work with Him. Picture a little boy tinkering in the garage helping his daddy fix the car. The boy learns to recognize the tools first, handing them to his dad as needed, and waits for the day when he's big enough to give them a try himself. He accumulates skill by spending hours watching, practicing under guidance, making an occasional error, and seeing how to correct it until the engine runs smoothly. If the boy never expresses any interest in learning what his father can teach him about car repair, then when he's older, he may break down on the side of the road and need to call him for help.

Our Father gladly teaches and disciplines us in preparation for more responsibility. If we refuse to pay attention to what God is doing and how He does it, our petitions to Him are usually cries for help. We either pretend we're prayer warriors just as children play cowboys and Indians, or we practice and learn from the Holy Spirit.

God waits patiently, celebrating with each small breakthrough. When we finally break down, during our darkest hours, we ask Christ to teach us the "how to" of prayer. There He teaches us not to place importance on the *how* of our faith, but rather W*hom* we believe. God is more interested in a relationship with us as we walk out our faith with Him rather than what we can accomplish through prayer. Our hardest choices and most embarrassing situations might reveal God's glory to others if we're honest. Are we watchful for such opportunities of faith when we pray? Are we ready for action when He reveals such a time?

Our faith lives in the certainty that Christ's Spirit resides in our flesh and breathes power into our words. If we really understand this truth, we use our tongue with extreme care. Cooperate with God and anticipate results in the spirit, not the flesh. Watch for people to draw nearer to Him, giving little concern to your own problems. Look for opportunities to work with Him because you're His son or daughter. Sometimes we receive physical healing, but we've asked for spiritual healing first. We do not need signs and wonders in this fleeting earthly realm, but we see hope springing out of despair and God's majesty working everywhere. Trusting God leads to a meaningful existence.

Trust in Him at all times, you people; pour out your heart before Him; God is a refuge for us. Surely men of low degree are a vapor, men of high degree are a lie; if they are weighed on the scales, they are altogether lighter than vapor. Do not trust in oppression, nor vainly hope in robbery; if riches increase, do not set your heart on them. God has spoken once, twice I have heard this: That power belongs to God. Also to You, O Lord, belongs mercy; for You render to each one according to his work.

Psalm 62:8

Turn off the noise around you and listen. When you sit alone in the quiet of your soul, your silence grows into a private conversation between God and you. Because you seek His righteousness, it usually turns out best if you let Him do most of the talking. His word created everything in the beginning. He can restore you and everyone you pray for.

Don't think that He's too busy for a relationship with you. He does not single out prayers with eloquent words and answer them first. He does not discriminate among the faithful. He responds in power to the unwavering determination of His people. He whispers to the weary in their sleep. The Holy Spirit groans on your behalf when you just don't know what to pray.[68]

Sometimes He wakes me up and urges me to open the Bible. He guides me to something specific and tenderly reveals a message, encouraging me with the realization that He knows what I need.

Toward the end of His ministry, Jesus summarized some amazing concepts about power over the flesh in **John 16 and 17**. He prepared the disciples to use the authority of His name when they prayed. In those days the disciples were powerful emissaries for Jesus. They led small groups, going out to heal and glorify God for all to see as they preached the message of Christ. Knowing that He would soon leave them, Jesus summoned them for some serious discussions. They needed to understand the foundation of spiritual works so that they could continue the job after His resurrection.

> **And in that day you will ask Me nothing. Most assuredly, I say to you, whatever you ask the Father in My name He will give you. Until now you have asked nothing in My name. Ask, and you will receive, that your joy may be full.**
>
> **John 16:23-24**

He went on to tell them that, although He had been demonstrating it for them, they would soon receive a direct connection to God himself.

> **These things I have spoken to you in figurative language; but the time is coming when I will no longer speak to you in figurative language, but I will tell you plainly about the Father.**
>
> **John 16:25**

Jesus laid out the spiritual side of the plan for mankind, literally explaining how He would provide access to Father God in the spiritual kingdom.

---

68   Romans 8:26-27

In that day you will ask in My name, and I do not say to you that I shall pray the Father for you; for the Father Himself loves you, because you have loved Me, and have believed that I came forth from God.

John 16:26-27

He plainly told them that they would need to take the relationship with Him to the next level by communicating with the Father too. Like most people today, they believed that God, in His holiness, kept His distance from them. Nice Jewish boys, they probably expected to connect with God indirectly during worship services, on Holy Days, and by hearing the Torah. They knew about the thick layered veil placed in the temple. It protected the priests from dying during a close encounter with God. Now Jesus told them they would approach the Creator just as they would their own father! Even after all these years, Christians know this in theory, but have trouble grasping this reality. Jesus explained how His Name, the key to this real connection with the Father, gave them authority in the heavenly realm.

To comprehend this better, let's briefly consider the limitation of Biblical translators as they described the multifaceted meanings of the Hebrew word for "God". When you see the word (God) in your Bible, it means more than we realize, sometimes referring to YHWH, the Sacred Name of G-d, the Creator of all beings and all things. HaShem is also translated "God" in our Bible, and literally means The Name; it is a replacement for the Sacred Name of YHWH. The Hebrew scribes, in this way, carefully protected the sanctity and accidental misuse of His Name. Yet at other times the translators used the word "God" and "Lord" when it refers to a whole class of spiritual creatures. When born again, we have the right to become part of this class of spirit-beings, too, with YHWY in control of His spiritual family.

When righteous sons and daughters take their place in God's family, they become a little higher than the angels.[69] When they use the Name of Christ with love, justice, truth, and mercy, certain angelic beings fall under

---

69   Ephesians 1:17-21

their authority. In other words, children of God practice using the new language of their eternal kingdom. We can function in that other world only because of Jesus' Name and only because the Father loves us.

The disciples understood they carried the power to cast out demons while He was alive, and Jesus wanted them to think about how this could continue after His body was gone. As hard as it was for the disciples to grasp this idea, Jesus knew that His indwelling Spirit would make it feasible. Next, He warned them not to see the coming earthly events as a defeat in their grief, and encouraged them to stay optimistic, regardless of the appearances.

These things I have spoken to you, that in Me you may have peace. In the world you will have tribulation; but be of good cheer, I have overcome the world.

John 16:33

Then He began to talk to the Father. He prayed for Himself, revealing His purpose:

Jesus spoke these words, lifted up His eyes to heaven, and said: "Father, the hour has come. Glorify Your Son, that Your Son also may glorify You, as You have given Him authority over all flesh, that He should give eternal life to as many as You have given Him. And this is eternal life, that they may know You, the only true God, and Jesus Christ whom You have sent."

John 17:1-3

Force yourself to pause here and consider what eternal life really means. We tend to think that eternal life begins at the end of our earthly life. We consider the word eternal from our own limited perspective of time and space. As I listen to this conversation where Christ Himself speaks to God Himself, both being One, the idea stimulates the measured particles of my brain and sparks my interest. Eternal life really begins at our spiritual rebirth into the community of God's chosen family, here and now.

Jesus draws us close to know God in the depths of His Being; not a casual friendship where we call on Him when we need something. In the same way that we watch and learn from our earthly parents, we learn to imitate Him. We pick up His habits and begin to grow toward our spiritual destiny. We see that our spiritual Father speaks with love and judgment in the same breath, at the same time. We could spend an entire lifetime studying that one aspect of Him, but it gradually becomes part of our identity too. Our old ways fade and selfish desires seem strangely far away.

We practice the art of mastery over our thoughts, words and actions more each day, as we follow Him into eternal life. We begin to understand what He expects, recognize His voice above the bad news all over the earth, and find ourselves working with Him as He builds the kingdom. We merge with His Spirit to the point that He fills us. With or without our flesh, the joy of searching the unknowable aspects of our limitless God goes on for eternity!

Then Jesus prayed to His Father for the disciples. Notice the key phrase about keeping God's word:

I have manifested Your name to the men whom You have given Me out of the world. They were Yours, You gave them to Me, and they have kept Your word. Now they have known that all things which You have given Me are from You. For I have given to them the words which You have given Me; and they have received *them,* and have known surely that I came forth from You; and they have believed that You sent Me.

John 17:6-8

Jesus outlined the specific way His obedience took shape when He walked the earth. He passed on the words of His Father as He heard them! Could it be any simpler? He gave them nothing complicated to memorize. He offered no method to learn in order to carry on His mission. Listen to His words, paying special attention to a prayer for our time as the nations flounder around us. He does not pray for the world.

I pray for them. I do not pray for the world but for those whom You have given Me, for they are Yours. And all Mine are Yours, and Yours are Mine, and I am glorified in them.

John 17:9-10

All mine are yours and yours are mine. As a disciple (follower) of Christ, I love that part. It anchors me in my relationships with others and connects them to my Father by His own design. It transfers all rights and privileges of children of God to believers, because look what Jesus said next. Remember, He was still talking to God.

But now I come to You, and these things I speak in the world, that they may have My joy fulfilled in themselves. I have given them Your word; and the world has hated them because they are not of the world, just as I am not of the world. I do not pray that You should take them out of the world, but that You should keep them from the evil one. They are not of the world, just as I am not of the world. Sanctify them by Your truth. Your word is truth.

John 17:13-17

Stop to consider why Jesus asked God to protect us from the evil one. Does God allow Satan's opposition as exercise for some eternal purpose? Yes, for now. If He allows it, why do we need protection? Well, someone needs to hold the hand of a toddler when they cross the street. It does not mean that cars are always dangerous, but until they learn the safety rules and mature in their ability to make decisions, children need supervision. Recognizing the evil one is part of our basic spiritual pre-school curriculum. The evil one jeopardizes generations lured into falsehood, but God protects His family during routine workouts when they turn to Him for guidance.

The real danger lies in cooperating with evil spirits by default or cowardice. Thus, we empower demons with our lack of understanding of the spiritual world where they function. Their voices sound vaguely familiar to us. "After all," they tell us, "you're sinners, never perfect, never worthy."

Worries creep into our minds as we pray, and then if God does not answer to our satisfaction, we begin to wonder why. "What if we have done something to offend God? What right do we have to expect a positive outcome?"

Do you see how easily the evil one slips his nagging ideas into our thoughts about prayer, calling us away from the kingdom of God's authority? We possess the power to rid ourselves of pessimism and feelings of helplessness by focusing on the word of God. Jesus knew this would be a great challenge for us and we would need to spend many hours in private time with Him to grasp it. His word guides us to separate ourselves from these spirits with His help. God gives us plenty of practice and rewards every step of obedience.

Jesus did not pray for us to be taken out of this physical world, but that God would protect us from evil with full, joyful hearts. We cannot depend on our feelings and emotions to protect us. Feelings of powerlessness and guilt try to steal our reward again and again. Our intellect cannot protect us in the spirit, but we must use our minds to imitate Christ and out-think the devil.

Jesus understood that our beliefs would lead to controversy, not popularity. Believing God, we take the narrow path, not the path of least resistance. After He prayed for Himself and the disciples, He prayed for you and me!

I do not pray for these (disciples) **alone, but also for those who will believe in Me through their word; that they all may be one, as You, Father, *are* in Me, and I in You; that they also may be one in Us, that the world may believe that You sent Me. And the glory which You gave Me I have given them, that they may be one just as We are one: I in them, and You in Me; that they may be made perfect in one, and that the world may know that You have sent Me, and have loved them as You have loved Me. Father, I desire that they also whom You gave Me may be with Me where I am, that they may behold My glory which You have given Me; for You loved Me before the foundation of the world.**
John 17:20-24

What a request! Read it again. "**May they** (all believers) **be one in Us** (Jesus and the Father) **that the world may believe!**" Jesus prayed that we would be brought to complete unity! Do you believe that God will answer the prayer of Jesus? Of all the prayers in the world, we know the fulfillment of this one continues to vibrate into eternity. It gives me such optimism and hope! Surely that's why He prayed aloud this time. He continues to sanctify us with the truth and we look for our part in it. Today, God speaks these words and they come alive to do a work in those He has chosen. I've asked Him to forgive me for participating in divisiveness. It's your turn. Spread the news. Ask Him to remove your blinders and teach you the truth.

Our willingness to believe God answered this prayer requires a leap of faith, however, because the fulfillment hinges on the cooperation of *all* true believers with varied doctrines and dogmas. It supersedes yesterday, today and tomorrow. As I write these words, the very sound of them makes me want to avoid the discomfort and controversy they bring into the church. They represent the most repellent doctrine to the vast majority of God's chosen people. However, as we enter the narrow door of the kingdom one by one, we find our place in a **unified body of holy citizens**.

Do we think or act as if any of this is true? Individually, we try to believe that God the Father, Jesus and His Spirit live in us, but do we live *in them* at the same time? I have tried to draw a diagram. I tried to match it up with our current understanding of physics. His living water floods my imagination. I drink it in and then I swim in it.

Ask Jesus to pray this prayer specifically for you. Put your name in it and pray it with Him. Pause and try to picture it for yourself. Believe in your all-encompassing and absolute connection to your Savior and Creator. Find the other sons of God regardless of their denomination, and understand that Jesus binds you as one congregation. He wants us to live abundant lives of purpose.

Jesus prayed: "**I desire that they also whom You gave Me may be with Me where I am, that they may behold My glory which You have given Me;**" This is the prayer of Jesus for you. In His presence, the light of His glory breaks through all feelings of hesitation. You see all creation rushing to follow His command.

If He tells the host of heaven that your thoughts and words are trustworthy and true, they must obey you. Demons will stand aside or plunge into the abyss. When you pray, your words carry the authority to make something happen. Because you spend time with His Son *where He is*, learning about righteousness, God commands His servants to carry out your requests.

THE LOVE OF YOUR LIFE

Take off your hiking boots and slip on your sandals for this segment. Enter the Rest with a pure heart and ask God to reveal something new about your relationship with Him. Discover eternity, one Today at a time. We've explored how He protects and teaches you as a caring father. But He also desires your mature companionship. He loves you as a true husband, and His depth of passion arouses your own desire for Him. On earth we glimpse His plan for us in the everlasting. He created delight as well as discipline, so extraordinary is the love He lavishes upon His believers who look to Him for comfort and joy.

In the Old Testament, *Song of Songs*, a tiny allegorical book of poetic grace, shows us just how much God cares for us. The Hebrew sages called it *The Holy of Holies*, the *Book of Communion*. We also know it as *The Song of Solomon*.

It tells of a love story laced in symbolism about Jesus, (the Shepherd King, the lover) and you, (the maiden, the beloved). It reveals mysterious facets of God's character. The story begins with your sense of separation and desire for your lover. This time of spiritual darkness and searching actually enhances the relationship, because you realize how much you need Him. Your anguish turns to ecstasy as you search for God and He satisfies the longings of your soul.

Embedded in the Old Testament, the book hints at the excitement of a personal bond with your Shepherd King. You call out to Him:

Tell me, O you whom I love, where you feed *your flock,* where you make *it* rest at noon. For why should I be as one who veils herself by the flocks of your companions?

Song of Songs 1:7

Notice the maiden's (your) desire to find Him away from the crowd. She instinctively knows she needs an unveiled, one-on-one reunion with Him. Ask the Holy Spirit to lead you to more intimate communion with your Messiah. Slip into your spirit to pursue your bridegroom, your savior, with abandon. Your soul bears you safely to your place in the kingdom of heaven as you stroll beneath a tree and sit in the shade to relax with Him.

Like an apple tree among the trees of the woods, so *is* my beloved among the sons. I sat down in his shade with great delight, and his fruit *was* sweet to my taste. He brought me to the banqueting house, and his banner over me *was* love.

Song of Songs 2:3-4

When you first read it you may blush at the unexpected sensual metaphors. While these words point to deep fulfillment as two lovers commit themselves to each other, ask the Holy Spirit to open a vision far beyond the flesh. This little surprise package from our God, the one who created us to be united as one flesh, unwraps many facets of adoration in the poetry of the lover and the beloved.

As they convey their desire to be together, they communicate the exclusiveness that makes their relationship sacred. But for now, I urge you to take a bite of the spiritual fruit that only Jesus offers from the tree of life. Read these passages as if they survived the ages just for you, the beloved, and your lover, the Shepherd King.

His left hand *is* under my head, and his right hand embraces me.

Song of Songs 2:6

He tenderly supports your thoughts, if you take the time to rest with your head in His arms and give your mind over to Him. He cares about your feelings and promises to wrap you in His love. You tell your friends,

Do not stir up nor awaken love until it pleases.

Song of Songs 2:7b

You instinctively know that your desire for Him builds, but you do not totally fall in love with Him until you are ready. No one else can push you into it or teach you about this relationship with your Lord. As you rest with the Shepherd King, He tells you,

Behold, you *are* fair, my love! Behold, you *are* fair! You *have* dove's eyes.

Song of Songs 1:15

Are you ready to receive that kind of unconditional love? You may say, "No, Lord, you must be thinking of someone else. My eyes are not always full of innocence and peace. I am not beautiful." The burden of shame makes it impossible to grasp this truth fully.

He seems to say to you, "I see that you sense our separation. Come closer and listen. You are like a lily among the thorns to me. The fact that you seek me makes me want to protect you. You are different from the others in the flock, standing out in perfect uniqueness to me. When you are ready for me, your love will be ripe with desire as you come to rest with me." Listen as He calls you to come out from your hiding place.

O my dove, in the clefts of the rock, in the secret *places* of the cliff, let me see your face, let me hear your voice; for your voice *is* sweet, and your face *is* lovely.

Song of Songs 2:14

As you continue to play hide and seek with Him, He speaks to you about your little habitual sins.

Catch us the foxes, the little foxes that spoil the vines, for our vines *have* tender grapes.

Song of Songs 2:15

These little foxes appear harmless, but they destroy the fruit of your garden when no one is watching. Why does He ask you to catch them? First He points out the obvious. Little erroneous patterns in your life seem like a natural part of the landscape. The cunning nocturnal foxes represent the sneaky or shady spirits in you, habitual sins you have made no effort to eradicate. They are small omissions and difficult to see, so you will need to outsmart them.

You must make the choice to get rid of the pests in your own spiritual garden if you want to live in the kingdom with Him. He reminds you of the adventure and makes it sound like a game. "Catch for *us* the foxes, the little foxes that ruin *our* vineyards." He wants you to take the initiative and now you suddenly *want* to change. He rejoices with you each time you capture one and declare victory over it!

You claim His love for yourself. He seems elusive, but as you prepare for Him in your heart, He waits and watches for you.

My beloved *is* mine, and I *am* his. He feeds *his flock* among the lilies. Until the day breaks and the shadows flee away, turn, my beloved, and be like a gazelle or a young stag upon the mountains of Bether.

Song of Songs 2:16-17

Now you know where to search for Him: feeding His flock among the lilies. His untamed spirit and unchanging nature cannot be defined. You begin the inner work of cleaning your spiritual landscape for Him. Often during sleepless nights of soul searching, you pray He will show up. You hope and wonder and wait.

By night on my bed I sought the one I love; I sought him, but I did not find him.

Song of Songs 3:1

Then, at some point in your life, perhaps in your darkest hour, you decide to get up and look for Him in earnest.

"I will rise now," *I said,* **"And go about the city; in the streets and in the squares I will seek the one I love." I sought him, but I did not find him. The watchmen who go about the city found me;** *I said,* **"Have you seen the one I love?"**

Song of Solomon 3:1-3

Driven almost to the point of desperation, you begin to look on your own. In this dim world, the spiritual streets crawl with demons, but you don't care. You'll risk your life (status quo) to find the truth at this point. You may take wrong turns but you actively seek Him. The watchmen find you as they make their rounds. Perhaps your watchmen are pastors, teachers or wise members of your community of faith. You ask them questions, but they can only tell you of the relationship they have with the Shepherd King. You must come to Him yourself.

Scarcely had I passed by them, when I found the one I love. I held him and would not let him go, until I had brought him to the house of my mother, and into the chamber of her who conceived me.

Song of Songs 3:4

You want to contain your relationship with Him in the boundaries of your own comfort zone. He gladly goes with you to meet your family and friends, and on a deeper level, you want to bring Him into your church. He made provisions for this need by creating the tabernacle within your heart where you can meet with Him regularly. As you go to meet with Him in the kingdom, you get a vision of the procession coming from afar. It is your King with the royal escort!

Behold, it *is* Solomon's couch, w*ith* sixty valiant men around it, of the valiant of Israel. They all hold swords, b*eing* expert in war. Every man *has* his sword on his thigh because of fear in the night.
Song of Songs 3:7-8

For the longest time you thought your relationship with God should be tucked away with your religious concept of faith. But now as you look closer, you see that He brings the carriage He made for Himself,

Its interior paved with love by the daughters of Jerusalem.
Song of Songs 3:10b

Never forget who built the carriage with love and faithfully carried the word of God, making it possible for each one of us to go with Him on the journey! Scripture continually reminds Christians of the exclusive connection we have to His chosen Hebrew people, and His desire for all of us to come to Him united as the family of Abraham. The warriors of the spiritual realm accompany you for protection.

Read for yourself as God reveals His love for your unique beauty and intricate features.

You have ravished my heart, my sister, *my* spouse; you have ravished my heart with one *look* of your eyes, with one link of your necklace... A garden enclosed i*s* my sister, *my* spouse, a spring shut up, a fountain sealed.
Song of Songs 4:9-12

His desire for a relationship with *you* brings closeness. Your time spent resting in the garden together grows into a deeper understanding of Him. Then you speak to the wind, His Spirit,

Awake, O north *wind,* *a*nd come, O south! Blow upon my garden, t*hat* its spices may flow out. Let my beloved come to his garden and eat its pleasant fruits.
Song of Songs 4:16

And He answers, this time inviting your friends and companions.

I have come to my garden, my sister, *my* spouse; I have gathered my myrrh with my spice; I have eaten my honeycomb with my honey; I have drunk my wine with my milk.

Song of Songs 5:1

The intoxicating joys of fellowship nourish you and give Him satisfaction too. He knows better than anyone about burning with passion. His relationship with the people who turn to Him is more valuable to Him than anything else He created. He wants us to love Him with our souls on fire.

Set me as a seal upon your heart, as a seal upon your arm; for love *is as* strong as death, jealousy *as* cruel as the grave; its flames *are* flames of fire, a most vehement flame. Many waters cannot quench love, nor can the floods drown it. If a man would give for love all the wealth of his house, it would be utterly despised.

Song of Songs 8:6-7

Stop and grasp the sheer life-changing force of God's kind of love. God says that He understands the yearning of our spirit. He created us to love Him. He pursues us, regardless of where we have been, to set our hearts on fire with His eternal flame! He places a seal upon us so that His servants will recognize us as part of the royal family.

I *am* my beloved's, and his desire *is* toward me. Come, my beloved, let us go forth to the field; let us lodge in the villages. Let us get up early to the vineyards; let us see if the vine has budded, w*hether* the grape blossoms are open, a*nd* the pomegranates are in bloom. There I will give you my love. The mandrakes give off a fragrance, and at our gates *are* pleasant *fruits,* a*ll manner,* new and old, which I have laid up for you, my beloved.

Song of Songs 7:10-13

186

When you look around and feel dissatisfied, turn off the noise, close out the chatter around you and tell God of your deepest longings. He has already prepared gifts especially for you. He loves you with tender intimacy and mysterious wisdom. He sees your spirit as a beautiful gazelle grazing among the lilies when no one else on earth seems to know you. You tremble with excitement at the thought of His unchanging love for you.

His allure is subtle. You do not understand its power. Why does He draw you near to Him? Is He jealous that you have ignored Him? He wants to awaken, yes even to arouse, the love He placed in your heart for Him. He wants you to come out of the trance that worldly desires have cast over your life and burn with passion for an *awareness* of His presence. He calls you into His vineyard to rest, to smell the fragrance of the blossoms.

TIME

The Bible tells us of a time before time began! God put signs in the sky as tools for us to measure our days on earth. Imagine His pure Spirit hovering, pulsating over the vast dark expanse of His earth. He created light on the first day to separate light from the darkness.

> **And God saw the light, that *it was* good; and God divided the light from the darkness.**
>
> **Genesis 1:4**

The more He created on this living canvas, the more He loved it, for He knew that His crowning creation would be fingers to touch, a nose to inhale the fragrance and eyes to feast on the glorious wonders of His creation. The depth and majesty of physical beauty pushed through into the intricate detail of each leaf. The source of each new life waited unseen in the hard lowly seed. Only God knew how wonderful these were! By the fourth day He said,

> **Then God said, "Let there be lights in the firmament of the heavens to divide the day from the night; and let them be for signs and seasons, and for days and years; and let them be**

for lights in the firmament of the heavens to give light on the earth"; and it was so.

Genesis 1:14-15

Although He already separated light from darkness, He positioned the sun, moon and the stars in the sky for identifying signs and seasons. He created time because He knew *we'd* need it. Our slow moving molecules would require a rhythm, a cadence to mark out our days on earth.

He appointed the moon for seasons; the sun knows its going down. You make darkness, and it is night, in which all the beasts of the forest creep about. The young lions roar after their prey, and seek their food from God. *When* the sun rises, they gather together and lie down in their dens. Man goes out to his work and to his labor until the evening.

Psalm 104:19-23

God knew that the spectacular lights in the sky would inspire and comfort as they measured out the time of man. The Word of God, our Jesus, participated at the beginning. The Bible tells us that God made all physical things through Him.

In the beginning was the Word, and the Word was with God, and the Word was God. He was in the beginning with God. All things were made through Him, and without Him nothing was made that was made. In Him was life, and the life was the light of men. And the light shines in the darkness, and the darkness did not comprehend it.

John 1:1-5

Jesus loved us before the beginning of time. So great was His passion to give us His light! So vast was His Spirit that He wanted us to experience it! So deeply He loved us that He created us to live with Him, not just for a time, but for eternity. All of this *before we came* to live on this earth. He loved us before we even knew of our own existence! Pause with me and think about that for a minute or two, and notice how freely we discuss what we will do with our time.

The Bible says there is a time for everything.

> **To everything *there is* a season,**
> **A time for every purpose under heaven:**
> **A time to be born, and a time to die;**
> **A time to plant, and a time to pluck *what is* planted;**
> **A time to kill, and a time to heal;**
> **A time to break down, and a time to build up;**
> **A time to weep, and a time to laugh;**
> **A time to mourn, and a time to dance;**
> **A time to cast away stones, and a time to gather stones;**
> **A time to embrace, and a time to refrain from embracing;**
> **A time to gain, and a time to lose;**
> **A time to keep, and a time to throw away;**
> **A time to tear, and a time to sew;**
> **A time to keep silence, and a time to speak;**
> **A time to love, and a time to hate;**
> **A time of war, and a time of peace.**

> **What profit has the worker from that in which he labors? I have seen the God-given task with which the sons of men are to be occupied. He has made everything beautiful in its time. Also He has put eternity in their hearts, except that no one can find out the work that God does from beginning to end.**

> **I know that nothing *is* better for them than to rejoice, and to do good in their lives, and also that every man should eat and drink and enjoy the good of all his labor—it *is* the gift of God. I know that whatever God does, it shall be forever. Nothing can be added to it, and nothing taken from it. God does *it,* that men should fear before Him.**

That which is has already been, and what is to be has already been; and God requires an account of what is past.

Ecclesiastes 3:1-15

God shapes our lives with appointed times for us to accomplish certain things for His own purpose. When Daniel was asked to explain Nebuchadnezzar's dream, he began by explaining where his insight originated.

Blessed be the name of God forever and ever, for wisdom and might are His. And He changes the times and the seasons; He removes kings and raises up kings; He gives wisdom to the wise and knowledge to those who have understanding. He reveals deep and secret things; He knows what *is* in the darkness, and light dwells with Him.

Daniel 2:20a-22

As we reflect on God's power to change our life, we know that real transformation begins with steps of obedience toward Him. Should we wait any longer to participate in God's kingdom? Every day that we procrastinate, we block the flow of purpose and energy that He ordains for us. We discover another repellent doctrine when we realize that **we live on borrowed time on earth**. We resist that idea as long as we live in the folly of our youth or in fear of change. He urges us to keep growing, as long as time remains. What does God want us to do with our days on earth?

Walk in wisdom toward those *who are* outside, redeeming the time. Le*t* your speech always *be* with grace, seasoned with salt, that you may know how you ought to answer each one.

Colossians 4:5-6

Who is "**outside**" the spiritual kingdom? Those who live in the flesh shall benefit from our **wisdom** if we live our lives caring about *their* eternal destiny. We flavor our conversations with true joy and sadness, expressing the realities of our time on earth as aliens and strangers. When we recognize our weaknesses as our greatest gifts, we tell others how Jesus' grace makes it possible to overcome. We point to God, the source of all good, and praise His name! Always be prepared with meaty, well-seasoned spiritual food for other hungry souls who might need encouragement.

The challenge remains for us to redeem the time, meaning that we should look for opportunities to share our story and tell about God's majesty in our lives. Watch for the chance to tell people the things of God that they specifically need to hear for their own edification and growth. Speak of God's redeeming love and grace to people gone astray. Distribute your blessings to the discouraged. Most of all, to those who are "outside", the unclean and untouchables in our communities, remember the mandate to love them in tangible ways that show them the generous nature of the One True Living God. Our time on earth remains valuable, priceless.

God carved the facets of His love so deeply into our spirits that they have the ability to reflect His light in a dark world. Think deeply, my brothers and sisters. Search back before time began and imagine a love so powerful and certain. Claim it for yourself. Claim it for your loved ones and friends. Claim it for your enemies and adversaries. Hang your every thought, word, and deed onto the reality of this truth. God appointed a time and place for each of us.

And He has made from one blood every nation of men to dwell on all the face of the earth, and has determined their pre-appointed times and the boundaries of their dwellings, so that they should seek the Lord, in the hope that they might grope for Him and find Him, though He is not far from each one of us; for in Him we live and move and have our being, as also some of your own poets have said, 'For we are also His offspring.'

Acts 17:26-28

God has long overlooked the ignorance of His offspring. We grope for Him, and He is not far off. That sums it up. The Old Testament overflows with expressions of God's frustration over the sinful choices of men.

People complained about His ways and quit trying to find Him. Yet His purpose stands forever, regardless of the opinions of men. God's word fills us with the hope that in Jesus we live and move and have our being. We are not accidents that waited to happen. We represent the offspring of God Himself, brothers and sisters of Christ.

> **Therefore, since we are the offspring of God, we ought not to think that the Divine Nature is like gold or silver or stone, something shaped by art and man's devising. Truly, these times of ignorance God overlooked, but now commands all men everywhere to repent, because He has appointed a day on which He will judge the world in righteousness by the Man whom He has ordained. He has given assurance of this to all by raising Him from the dead.**
>
> **Acts 17:29-31**

There's that word *repent* again. It's the common thread that pulls us all close to Him. While there's time, He offers new beginnings to those who turn away from the world and back to Him. It's not a suggestion, but a command, for **all men everywhere**. How vast is the depth of this realization that our salvation was planned before the creation of man![70] Many times when we see "repent", it refers to a 180-degree turn, but we learn that this word for repent translates from Greek root words **"meta and noeo, meaning with understanding"**[71]. As we pray for a purposeful grasp of our time on earth, we see that we are just souls passing through together. From here forward, Today, we must look around with understanding and see each life we touch through eyes of love.

> **Lord, You have been our dwelling place in all generations. Before the mountains were brought forth, or ever You had formed the earth and the world, even from everlasting to everlasting, You *are* God. You turn man to destruction, and say, "Return, O children**

---

70   Ephesians 1:3-5, Titus 1:2
71   Strong's - "meta" G3326 and "noeo" G3539, Condensed Brown-Driver-Briggs Hebrew Lexicon, Thayer's Greek Lexicon

of men." For a thousand years in Your sight *are* like yesterday when it is past, and *like* a watch in the night. You carry them away *like* a flood; *they are* like a sleep. In the morning they are like grass *which* grows up: In the morning it flourishes and grows up; in the evening it is cut down and withers. For we have been consumed by Your anger, and by Your wrath we are terrified. You have set our iniquities before You, our secret *sins* in the light of Your countenance. For all our days have passed away in Your wrath; we finish our years like a sigh.

The days of our lives *are* seventy years; and if by reason of strength *they are* eighty years, yet their boast *is* only labor and sorrow; for it is soon cut off, and we fly away. Who knows the power of Your anger? For as the fear of You, *so is* Your wrath. So teach *us* to number our days, that we may gain a heart of wisdom. Return, O LORD! How long? And have compassion on Your servants. Oh, satisfy us early with Your mercy, that we may rejoice and be glad all our days!

Make us glad according to the days *in which* You have afflicted us, the years *in which* we have seen evil. Let Your work appear to Your servants, and Your glory to their children. And let the beauty of the LORD our God be upon us, and establish the work of our hands for us; yes, establish the work of our hands.

Psalm 90

The time we spend on earth unfolds as a divine mystery. We may think about these things for a time, seeking further wisdom. We don't need to understand time, but we need to use it as a tool of measurement, a gift from our God, who sees a thousand years as one day. He asks that as we measure our days, we remember this:

But this I say, brethren, the time *is* short.

1 Corinthians 7:29a

Today, the words of our mouth and the work of our hands are useful to God as instruments of love. Let us burn with desire for Him. Let us be wise with the little knowledge we possess. Let us be grateful for the gifts we now have, and share them as if there is no more time.

Before He started His ministry, the Spirit drove Jesus into the wilderness where He fasted, prayed and practiced overcoming the devil. The Angels ministered to Him. Afterwards, He heard about John the Baptist's imprisonment and He interpreted it as a sign that the power and authority of God was imminent:

> **The time is fulfilled and the kingdom of God is at hand. Repent, and believe in the gospel.**
>
> **Mark 1:15b**

When you experience a crisis of faith, you may wonder if God is running late. Remember that His timing is perfect. While you're in the wilderness trying to brush off temptations from the devil, ask Jesus to teach you to master your flesh. Repent if you did not believe it was possible. Start there, and pray that His Spirit will lead you into the kingdom of God.

We live in a time of worldly chaos. Scientists track asteroids hurling to earth and terrorists plot to kill their enemies. Even non-believers understand that the prophecy of the end times seems plausible in our dangerous nuclear age.

> **And those of the people who understand shall instruct many; yet *for many* days they shall fall by sword and flame, by captivity and plundering. Now when they fall, they shall be aided with a little help; but many shall join with them by intrigue. And *some* of those of understanding shall fall, to refine them, purify *them*, and make *them* white, *until* the time of the end; because *it is* still for the appointed time.**
>
> **Daniel 11:33-35**

Although we possess a little insight, we often fall down anyway. Remember that God intends to use that experience. It is not the end of the world, even though it may seem that way. Only God can take our weakness, our self-centered depths, and turn up the fire to refine and purify us. Count yourself blessed when He does.

For those who refuse Him, however, there is still a time appointed by God when all of our human activity will change. At that time, when God abolishes sin,[72] pure wisdom will fill the thoughts of men.

We know from scripture that it will be a time of peace and perfection on earth. Illness, suffering, death and mourning will disappear. The old order of things will pass away. The spirits of all who love God will ascend with the all-encompassing love of the Holy Spirit. All others will experience the nothingness of separation from their Creator by choice. For now, we live with a promise and a warning:

Therefore, since a promise remains of entering His rest, let us fear lest any of you seem to have come short of it. For indeed the gospel was preached to us as well as to them; but the word which they heard did not profit them, not being mixed with faith in those who heard _it_.

Hebrews 4:1-2

When we believe the promise of the gospel, we follow Him into God's Rest. As we let go of our worldly strife, we realize that we live in the time of God's seventh day of creation. We live in a time and place where God continues to invite us into His kingdom. He is expecting us. He warns us to drop our self-importance and forget about earning our way to heaven. Jesus opened the Way into the kingdom. He calls us to a faith that brings us to our knees, and then moves us into action. All for Him. We need nothing but the wisdom to follow closely.

Then, we must put away _our ideas_ of what we should do and listen closely for _God's idea_ for us. He invites us to do something at the appointed time. The ripple effect of our obedience will last for eternity. He will put

---

72 Revelation 21:3-4

people in our lives Today. Is God calling you into a deeper relationship with them? Do they need to feel the warmth of His powerful love?

"No, Lord, I don't have time," we may have once said. Today our answer will be different.

Today we feel a breeze and we hear God whisper that we have borrowed His tools. Time, we recall, is a tool He devised so we could measure our life on earth.

"Time," He laughs. "One of my favorite tools! Use it for the family business!"

To this day, we experience the undeniable elements of His love and feel the warmth of His grace. "It is enough," He seems to remind us. "Come in... there is enough for everyone."

CPSIA information can be obtained
at www.ICGtesting.com
Printed in the USA
LVHW112109190223
739905LV00005B/174